PASSENGER SHIPS OF THE IRISH SEA

—

1919-1969

LAURENCE LIDDLE

COLOURPOINT BOOKS

Designed by Colourpoint Books, Newtownards

Printed by ColourBooks

ISBN 1 898392 30 7

Colourpoint Books

Unit D5, Ards Business Centre
Jubilee Road
NEWTOWNARDS
Co Down
N Ireland
BT23 4YH
Tel: (01247) 820505 / 819787 Ex 239
Fax: (01247) 821900
E-mail: info@colourpoint.co.uk
Web-site: www.colourpoint.co.uk

Front cover:
Cambria berthed at Dun Laoghaire on 14 July 1963.

John Langford

Frontispiece:
The British Rail motor ship *Hibernia*, 4972 grt, 397' x 54', built by Harland and Wolff in 1949, backing away from Carlisle Pier, Dun Laoghaire, en route to Holyhead. The ship is using the former arrival side of the pier.

Sean Kennedy/Green studios

ACKNOWLEDGEMENTS

    I state, in the introduction to this book, that what I have to tell is based very largely on memory but that I have also drawn on some reading and correspondence. Apart from many volumes of *Lloyds' Register* (consulted by courtesy of the Librarian and staff of the Australian National Maritime Museum), my written sources have included two articles published in the *Journal of the Irish Railway Record Society*: 'Irish Sea Railway Steamers' by the late H M Rea, in Journal No 22 and 'Rosslare Harbour' by Oliver Doyle, in issues 42 and 43. Books which have either provided information or have enabled me to check details are: *Across the Irish Sea*, a history of the Belfast Steamship Co, by Dr Robert Sinclair; *Down the Quay*, the story of the port of Dundalk, compiled by a group of young people from that town; *The Long Watch*, by Captain Frank Forde, a former commodore master of the British and Irish Line, an account of the operations and losses of Irish ships during the Second World War; *Northwards by Sea*, a history of the North of Scotland and Orkney and Shetland Steam Navigation Company, by the late Professor Gordon Donaldson; and *Sealink* by Brian Haresnape.

I have benefited from correspondence with Dr H S Corran and Dr D B McNeill, both of whom have also been helpful with photographs, and also with Alan Browne, John O'Neill and Dr Robert Sinclair. I am particularly grateful to Alan Brown for encouraging me to write this account of Irish Sea services, and to John O'Neill for having given me a copy of *Down the Quay*, a book which I might not otherwise have come across.

The original draft of the first section of the book (though considerably shorter than what I have written here) appeared as 'Railway Passenger Steamers on the Irish Sea', in issues No 123 and 124 of the *Journal of the Irish Railway Record Society*. I am indebted to Mr Kevin Murray, editor of the Journal, for permission to use that article as the basis for the first part of the present work.

I owe special thanks to Norman and Sheila Johnston of Colourpoint Books who, after a number of successful publications dealing with land transport, have with the present volume launched their first maritime enterprise. My best thanks are due also to everyone who has helped with photographs, both in supplying prints and in indicating where prints might be found. Their assistance has been a vital element in the production of the book.

I have noted the sources of all photographs and extend my warmest thanks to all those persons and organisations who have provided them. As regards organisations, I would like to mention the help of Stephen Rabson and Lyn Palmer, of P and O (as successors to Coast Lines), and of my good friend David Murray of the Irish Railway Record Society and of another fellow railway devotee, Robin Morton of the Belfast Telegraph. I am grateful too to Barry Carse for permission to use colour photographs taken by his late father, Sam, and to Nelson Poots who was instrumental in locating the *Princess Victoria* pictures. Although his name appears below the relevant pictures, a special word of thanks must go to Sean Kennedy for his photograph of the *Connaught* (not forgetting the crew's laundry!). This illustration of one of the old City of Dublin 'Mail Boats', is by far the best I have ever seen of any member of that memorable quartet.

Finally, I must mention the considerable influence which my father, the late Laurence Henry Liddle, had on the early development of my interest in ships and sea travel. He was ever patient in answering a small boy's many questions (eg "How big are the propellers of the *Hibernia*?"), and provided much information, and not a few good stories from his own travel experiences, not only on the Irish Sea, but also from passages to and from Shetland, in the very early years of the present century. His tale of the mate of one of the 'North Company's' ships having to go over the side in order to eject, by means of a long handled mop, through a porthole, a passenger who had immured himself in the 'Gents' will always remain green in my memory.

Laurence Liddle

January 1998

> *To JKL comes carissima multos per annos.*

Laurence Liddle, a retired Chartered Surveyor, was born at Howth, near Dublin, in 1915. His early interest in ships grew out of many visits to Howth harbour and regular childhood holidays to England using the Dun Laoghaire mail steamers.

This interest in ships was reinforced by a period of residence in Scotland in the 1930s, necessitating frequent trips back to Ireland. His professional career involved regular travel by ship between Ireland and Britain, during which he sampled every route and virtually every ship.

Mr Liddle is a Fellow of the Royal Institute of Chartered Surveyors and other professional bodies. He is a long-standing member of the Irish Railway Record Society and a past Chairman of the Railway Preservation Society of Ireland, and has contributed numerous articles to the Journals of both these organisations, as well as to the shipping periodical *Sea Breezes*. He is also author of *Steam Finale*, a book of Irish railway footplate memories (IRRS London 1964).

CONTENTS

THE BACKGROUND

In the autumn of 1933, my mother, travelling overnight from Dublin to Glasgow in the Burns and Laird Lines' vessel *Lairdsmoor*, asked a stewardess if she might have a bath. The stewardess said, "Yes, the passenger might certainly have a bath", and indicated the whereabouts of the bathroom. My mother proceeded to the designated apartment, only to be taken more than somewhat aback on discovering that the bath was, if not full of, at least partially stacked with loaves of bread. She did not get her bath.

This trivial story illustrates two points of difference between Irish Sea passenger services of pre 'car ferry' days and those currently in operation. The first is that services then were not concentrated on just the short sea routes; the second is that for first class passengers hotel standards were at least aimed at, even if they were not always achieved in the *Lairdsmoor*.

The following pages outline the main passenger services across the Irish Sea which operated from the end of the First World War until ro-ro vessels succeeded 'conventional' ships in the 1960s and early 1970s. What I have written here has been based mostly on memory and does not claim to be a comprehensive history; rather it embodies recollections of many crossings of the Irish Sea and of quay-side saunterings, mostly in Dublin, supplemented by some reading, conversations and correspondence. Although the period covered is basically the half century after 1919 I have not felt myself rigidly bound to dates, and hence the reader will find occasional references to earlier or later years, particularly as regards vessels built before or surviving after my main period. I have said relatively little about services during the Second World War or of the wartime careers of the many Irish Sea vessels which operated in unfamiliar waters between 1939 and 1945. I have made some reference to the Irish Sea routes and their ships during the war years, but because a history of the doings of Irish Sea vessels in wartime would provide the material for a sizable book in its own right, and also because my opportunities for cross channel travel and harbour excursions were greatly restricted during the first half of the 1940s, what I have written is mainly concerned with peacetime operations.

Operating Groups

Between 1919 and 1969 the very great majority of sea passenger services between Britain and Ireland were operated by one or other of two groups, the railway companies and the Coast Lines combine.

THE RAILWAY COMPANIES' SERVICES

At the beginning of our period the London and North Western, the Great Western, the Lancashire and Yorkshire and the Portpatrick and Wigtownshire Joint Railways all ran shipping services directly. The Great Western of England and the Great Southern and Western of Ireland jointly owned the Fishguard and Rosslare Railways and Harbours Company, whose steamers were operated by the Great Western, whilst the North British, which owned the docks at Silloth in the north west of England, had an interest in the service between Dublin, Douglas (Isle of Man) and Silloth, which was worked by the Glasgow firm of William Sloan and Company.

After the grouping of the railway companies in Britain at the beginning of the year 1923 (the London and North Western and the Lancashire and Yorkshire had amalgamated in the previous year), the enlarged London and North Western, the Midland and the Portpatrick and Wigtownshire companies, along with others which need not concern us here, merged into the London Midland and Scottish (hereafter referred to as the LMS), whilst the North British became an important constituent of the London and North Eastern (LNER). The Great Western was so much the predominant partner in its group that its name was retained as the title of the new organisation. None of the other companies in this group had any Irish shipping interests, though the Cambrian Railway had at one time had some involvement in a shipping service between Aberdovey and Wexford. The Fishguard and Rosslare Railways and Harbours Company kept its lengthy title and its joint British and Irish parentage, although in 1925 the Great Southern and Western became the main constituent of the newly formed Great Southern Railways.

On 1 January 1948 the four British railway groups were nationalised as British Railways, This takeover included the ships, docks and other marine assets of the groups. The subsequent metamorphosis of British Railways' marine activities into 'Sea-Link', and the eventual sale of the latter to outside interests occurred for the most part after the establishment of ro-ro services, and lie largely outside the limits of our story.

THE COAST LINES

The Coast Lines concern which, under its own name, operated numerous cargo services around Britain and carried passengers on its Liverpool-London

W Grogan

The Clyde Shipping Company's *Rockabill*, 1392grt, 271'5"x 27'2", built on the Clyde by D and W Henderson in 1931. This ship was one of three cargo/livestock vessels, each with accomodation for twelve passengers, which maintained the Waterford-Liverpool and Waterford-Bristol services in the later inter-war years. For an example of a Clyde Shipping Company's ship with a greater passenger capacity see the pictures of *Rathlin/ Lairdscraig/Glengarriff*, on page 120.

route, owed its origin to a fusion of the former Powell and Hough lines. During and after the 1914-1918 war the company expanded considerably and absorbed, amongst others, the Belfast Steamship Company, the Burns Line (G and J Burns), the Laird Line (Alexander Laird and Company), the British and Irish Steam Packet Company and the City of Cork Steam Packet Company. Services operated by the Tedcastle Line between Dublin and Liverpool were also acquired, as were some routes of the City of Dublin Steam Packet Company. There were also acquisitions of two minor companies which will be referred to briefly later. In 1927 the Burns and the Laird Companies, each of which was based in Glasgow, amalgamated within the combine to become Burns and Laird Lines. The Belfast Steamship Company, the British and Irish Steam Packet Company and the City of Cork Steam Packet Company each retained its name, but the City of Dublin and the Tedcastle concerns lost their identities within the British and Irish.

There were therefore, from the later 1920s onward, four nominally independent companies, other than the railways, running passenger services between Britain and Ireland. However, apart from the fact that Coast Lines was the sole owner of all four organisations there were many signs of their common parentage. One indication was the frequent interchange of vessels, usually with appropriate change of names. Another, from 1929 onwards, was the development of a standard type of passenger/cargo ship, ultimately used by all four subsidiaries, whilst a third, minor perhaps but easily apparent to passengers, was the common uniform of dark blue jackets with purple lapels on which was the logo of intertwined shamrock, rose and thistle, worn by all stewards. This device also appeared on all plates, cups and saucers.

Coast Lines became a unit of the Royal Mail Group, to which the Belfast shipbuilding firm of Harland and Wolff also belonged. This connection led to the appearance of the standard type of vessel just referred to, of which thirteen were built, twelve by Harlands and one by Denny Brothers of Dunbarton.

THE CLYDE SHIPPING COMPANY

The Glasgow based Clyde Shipping Company operated an extensive network of cargo and cargo/livestock services between Glasgow/Ardrossan-Belfast/English south coast ports and London; Glasgow-Belfast/Dublin/Waterford and Cork; Waterford-Bristol; Waterford-Liverpool and Glasgow-Limerick. However, although almost all of this company's ships had some passenger accommodation and were popular with summer holiday makers, the Clyde concern was not a significant factor in Ireland to Britain passenger traffic, and so is not dealt with here. The company played a very important role in the Irish livestock export trade, but that is another story.

THE ISLE OF MAN STEAM PACKET COMPANY

My original plan for this book was for it to deal only with the British/Irish services of the railway companies and those of the Coast Lines combine. However, it has been suggested to me that some reference to the ships and services of 'The Steam Packet' as it was commonly referred to, would interest readers. Consequently, I have added a short section dealing with the island company.

Since, however, I have made a total of just three passages in Isle of Man ships, compared to over one hundred and fifty in railway and Coast Lines vessels, I have very little personal travel experience to draw on. Moreover, such experience as I have relates to a time long after the main period covered in the book. Also, the fact that both Dublin and Belfast, the locations of most of my quayside saunterings, were served by just a limited number of IOMSP Co vessels, and those only during the summer, ensured that my land based observations of the red and black funnelled 'miniature Cunarders' were also limited.

Nevertheless, because the successive *Mona's Queens*, *King Orrys*, *Ben my Chrees* and their sisters were very definitely passenger ships of the Irish Sea it is only reasonable that they should receive a mention.

THE RAILWAY COMPANIES' ROUTES

At the start of our period the individual railway companies and the Irish routes which they operated were as follows:

Portpatrick and Wigtownshire Joint Railway	Stranraer—Larne	London and North Western Railway	Holyhead—Dublin
London and North Western and Lancashire and Yorkshire Railways jointly	Fleetwood—Belfast	London and North Western Railway	Holyhead— Dun Laoghaire *(Kingstown)*
Midland Railway	Heysham—Belfast	Fishguard and Rosslare Railways and Harbours Company	Fishguard—Rosslare
Lancashire and Yorkshire Railway	Liverpool—Drogheda		
		Great Western Railway	Fishguard–Waterford
London and North Western Railway	Holyhead—Greenore	North British Railway *(a minor interest only)*	Silloth—Dublin

As well as passengers, cargo and livestock were carried by all of these services except that between Holyhead and Dun Laoghaire.

POST GROUPING

The grouping of Britain's railways, in 1923, led to alterations and reductions in their Irish shipping services. The Fleetwood-Belfast route was abandoned in 1928, whilst, in the same year, the service between Liverpool and Drogheda was taken over by the British and Irish section of Coast Lines. Passenger facilities were withdrawn from the Holyhead-Greenore route in 1927.

Consolidation of the services to Belfast from Fleetwood and Heysham was an obvious economy. The Holyhead and Greenore service, which had been established by the London and North Western Railway Company in the 1870s, in an attempt to increase its share of the traffic to and from the north of Ireland, had never been a great success. It became even less so after the partition of Ireland in 1921. It was only logical that the Liverpool-Drogheda route should go to Coast Lines rather than continue to be worked by the LMS. Liverpool was not a railway port, but it housed the headquarters of the entire Coast Lines group.

The LNWR's express passenger services between Holyhead and Dublin/ Dun Laoghaire (known as Kingstown until 1922) were rationalised in 1919-20, after the railway company had successfully tendered for the operation of the mail service to and from Dun Laoghaire — a service which for many years had been the preserve of the City of Dublin Steam Packet Company. The most important act of rationalisation was the abandonment of the first class express route between Holyhead and Dublin (North Wall). However the resulting lack of a 'prestige' service direct from the City of Dublin to Britain was to a considerable degree made good afterwards, when Coast Lines (British and Irish Steam Packet Co) greatly improved the Liverpool-Dublin connection.

Neither of the two services based on Fishguard was abandoned after 1919, although there were reductions in frequencies compared to those of pre-war days. The quasi-railway route between Silloth and Dublin underwent no significant change.

Individual Railway Services

It is now time for us to consider each of the railway-owned passenger services.

STRANRAER-LARNE

Throughout our period the Stranraer-Larne connection operated once daily six days a week all the year round, with an extra daily sailing each way during the summer in peacetime. In the 1920s the regular vessels were *Princess Maud*, 1746 gross registered tons (grt), 301′x 40′, built in 1904 and *Princess Victoria*, 1687 grt, 301′x 40′, which dated from 1912. These ships, built by Denny Brothers of

National Library of Ireland

The triple-screw turbine steamer *Princess Maud*, built by Denny's of Dumbarton in 1904, leaving Larne. The date of the photograph is some time before 1923, as the ship has the all yellow funnels of the Portpatrick and Wigtownshire Joint Railway, rather than the post-grouping buff with black top of the LMS.

National Library of Ireland

This picture of the first *Princess Victoria*, built in 1912 by Dennys (who were specialists in the construction of cross channel turbine steamers) shows the buff black-topped funnels adopted by the LMS. The vessel is alongside the quay at Larne.

Dunbarton, were of the standard early twentieth century express cross-channel type, powered by direct drive steam turbines operating triple screws. They had the usual long midship structure one deck high, open side decks and twin funnels. Two classes of passenger were carried, first class (commonly designated **saloon**), in relative luxury amidships, and third class (designated **steerage**), in considerable discomfort in the stern. *Princess Maud* was withdrawn in 1931 and *Princess Victoria* in 1934.

Passenger facilities from and to Stranraer were greatly improved in 1931 with the advent of the *Princess Margaret*, 2552 grt, 325′x 47′2″, which had geared turbines driving twin screws giving a service speed of 20½ knots. Like her predecessors and the great majority of railway-owned vessels, this coal fired, single funnelled ship was built by Dennys.

For the most of the thirty years following her introduction the *Princess Margaret* was the mainstay of the Stranraer-Larne service, even though in 1934 she was joined by a near sister, *Princess Maud*, 2883 grt, 330′x 49′. Each of these ships carried first and third class passengers, mails, general cargo (which included a heavy railway parcels traffic) and a limited number of livestock. Steerage accommodation, situated aft, was of the somewhat spartan standard of the day, but saloon passengers were very well catered for in public rooms liberally provided with the mahogany and carpets of the period. In each ship, on the boat deck forward there was a glassed-in observation shelter, whilst at the after end of the same deck was the first class smoking room/bar. Below the boat deck the main deck, with fully open sides in *Princess Margaret* but plated in forward in *Princess Maud*, had a lounge, purser's bureau and some sleeping cabins forward and a dining saloon and galley aft. Below this deck there was more sleeping accommodation.

From 1931 to 1934 the *Princess Margaret*, relieved as necessary by the elderly *Princess Victoria*, maintained the basic service, leaving Stranraer around 0700 after the arrival of the through London train, and berthing at Larne at about 0915. The ship left on the return service at about 1900 and was due back at her home port some 2¼ hours later, after a passage of "only seventy minutes open sea", as the contemporary advertising slogan announced. There were tight rail connections at each port to and from London, Belfast and Glasgow, except that passengers travelling from the latter city had to do so by a train which departed at around 2100 on the evening before sailing, and which arrived at Stranraer at midnight. They were then faced with a seven hour wait on board before the vessel left the quay. This situation was by no means ideal, whether one bedded down in an armchair or on a sofa, or recklessly squandered two shillings and sixpence (12½p) for a made up bed in a two-berth cabin. If when travelling to Glasgow one was deterred by the prospect of arriving by train in that city at midnight it was possible to expend the same modest sum and remain in one's berth until 0600 the next day, resuming the journey by an early morning train.

However, there were drawbacks to sleeping on board at Stranraer. Cargo working went on intermittently during the night, making sleep difficult to achieve. Nevertheless the cabin ventilation in *Princess Margaret*, by forced draught, through adjustable nozzles, was a great improvement on the provision (or lack of provision) of air in the older ships. Be it noted that these remarks on sleeping accommodation refer to facilities for saloon passengers. I have travelled steerage in both *Princess Maud* and *Princess Margaret*, but since on each occasion I was travelling straight through to the north of England I can offer no personal experience of how third class passengers fared during the night watches at Stranraer.

Between 1934 and 1939 the *Princess Maud* was the main service ship. *Princess Margaret* provided the extra summer sailings, at around 0900 ex-Larne and 1800 ex-Stranraer, relieved *Princess Maud* as required and also did some relief work and extra sailings on the Heysham-Belfast route. In 1939 the twin screw diesel-engined *Princess Victoria*, 2500 grt, 301'x 48', the first ro-ro (roll-on/roll-off) ship built for Irish Sea services, was delivered by Dennys and took over the extra summer sailings, the *Princess Margaret* being permanently (so it was thought at the time) transferred to Heysham. Despite some differences in the layout of the passenger accommodation, necessitated by the provision of space for vehicles, the external appearance of the new vessel was very similar to that of *Princess Maud* and *Princess Margaret*. Like the Harwich and Dover based train ferries and her own ill-fated namesake and successor, the *Princess Victoria* had an open stern at vehicle deck level, with half height doors which afforded merely a psychological protection against the sea.

The new ship was taken over by the British Government at the start of the war, but was lost in 1940. For some periods during the war years the *Princess Maud* served on her old route, often acting as a troop carrier between Scotland and Northern Ireland. As an LSI (Landing Ship Infantry) she was involved in the Normandy landings. *Princess Maud* was converted to burn oil fuel in 1946 and, early in 1947, was transferred to the Holyhead-Dun Laoghaire service. She regularly reappeared at Larne and Stranraer as a relief to *Princess Margaret* and also worked occasional Heysham-Belfast 'extras' during the summer. A regular example of an 'extra', in the 1950s and early 1960s, was to provide a second evening sailing ex-Belfast on the Friday before the start of the Northern Ireland July holidays. In British Rail days the ship ran once or twice between Fishguard and Rosslare and Fishguard and Waterford and, during the summer of 1951, worked between Southampton and Saint Malo.

However, despite these occasional 'foreign' excursions, for most of her last eighteen years *Princess Maud* was a Holyhead ship, in which guise I came to know her better than I had done during her Stranraer days. It would be fair to say that during the 1950s and 1960s, as the standby vessel for the Dun Laoghaire service, for which two 4900 ton motor ships had been built in 1949, she suffered greatly by comparison with her running mates and was endured, rather than extolled, by the travelling public. For my part, as a ship enthusiast I was always

World Ship Society

The *Princess Maud*, built by Dennys in 1934 for the LMS Railway's Larne-Stranraer service, is pictured here at Holyhead after she had been transferred permanently to that port in 1947, to serve as the relief vessel on the Holyhead-Dun Laoghaire route.

happy to cross the Irish Sea in her. *Princess Maud* was sold to eastern Mediterranean buyers in 1964 and appeared in the 1965 Lloyds' Register as the *Venus*, 3032 grt.

The *Princess Margaret*, which returned to Stranraer at the beginning of the war, was converted to oil burning in 1952 and continued to operate on the route for which she had been built until 1962, when she was replaced by the turbine ro-ro vessel *Caledonian Princess*. The old ship went to Hong Kong owners who renamed her *Macau* and, after extensive alterations, put her on the service from Hong Kong to the Portuguese enclave of Macau. In 1971 the former *Princess Margaret* was driven ashore by typhoon Rose and was subsequently scrapped, forty years after her first appearance at Stranraer.

During the later years of their careers both *Princess Maud* and *Princess Margaret* had their third class accommodation upgraded. Among other improvements the salon bar on the former vessel was given over to steerage passengers, whilst, in the case of her sister, the same apartment became a first class restaurant, the former 'saloon dining room' being redesignated 'third class'. To compensate for the loss of saloon bar accommodation in each ship, the forward observation shelters on the boat decks became bars.

These two 'Princesses' were well appointed ships, particularly so in view of the short passages for which they had been designed. The Stranraer-Larne service was extensively advertised as 'The Short Sea Route' and not only carried a fairly heavy all the year round traffic between the north of Ireland and Scotland and England, but also between the south of the country and Scotland. (I once came across a traveller making his way from Dublin to London by this route, but that was surely exceptional.)

However, with full load draughts of only 11'8" for *Princess Margaret* and 11'6" in the case of *Princess Maud*, these ships were notorious rollers. For saloon passengers, excellent breakfasts and evening meals were available but, on occasions, weather conditions in the North Channel (a NW or SE gale, against an ebb or flowing tide respectively, for example) precluded their consumption, at least in any degree of comfort. I have a vivid recollection of one such occasion. Early in 1938, I crossed from Stranraer to Larne in the *Princess Margaret* (no doubt *Princess Maud* was undergoing her annual survey). The weather was such that the degree of acrobatic expertise needed to consume breakfast was rather greater than a landsman, such as myself, possessed. However, I was not too perturbed, since I was scheduled to travel straight through to Belfast by the boat train from Larne and thence onwards by the 1030 Dublin express. This latter train had a very good buffet car service, so I reckoned that the pangs of hunger, though possibly rather long drawn out, would eventually be assuaged in an entirely satisfactory manner. Unfortunately, I had forgotten that there was an international rugby match being played in Dublin that day. There was not a seat to be had on the train, which was bearable, though disappointing. What was far worse was that it was impossible to get anywhere near the buffet car!

A somewhat pleasanter recollection of the *Princess Margaret* dates from the

1950s, when my wife and I and our two sons travelled on one of the regular day trips operated from Larne, on the occasion of the annual holiday in that town. On a fine summer day we steamed to and around Ailsa Craig. On board it was open house and, during most of the time, there were queues lined up for conducted visits to bridge and engine room.

During the war years the Stranraer-Larne route carried very heavy civilian and military traffic and I have already noted that, whilst *Princess Margaret* was the mainstay of the civilian service between 1939 and 1945 (though I travelled on *Princess Maud* in that role early in 1942), her sister served both as a troop carrier between her peacetime ports and also in a more active military role. However, the exigencies of military traffic led to many strangers appearing on the short sea route, including a turbine vessel from the LMS Clyde Coast services, a Thames excursion steamer and one of the Dover-Dunkirk train ferry ships.

The Stranraer-Larne service was the first of the Irish Sea routes to receive new tonnage after the war, in the shape of the ro-ro vessel *Princess Victoria*, 3694 grt, 308'8"x 48'1", a very similar ship to the one which had been lost in 1940. Dennys were again the builders, and the delivery year was 1946.

The new *Princess Victoria* (the third of the name) did not take up duty on the main all the year round service, which remained the preserve of the faithful *Princess Margaret*. Instead, the newcomer was set to work on the summertime extra morning sailing from Larne and evening return from Stranraer. More importantly however, the *Princess Victoria* operated many sailings for the transport of milk tankers between Northern Ireland and Scotland. She also relieved *Princess Margaret* as required.

THE PRINCESS VICTORIA DISASTER, 1953

However, it is not as milk boat, nor as a conveyor of tourists' cars and caravans, that the *Princess Victoria* is still remembered over forty years after her name disappeared from the pages of Lloyds' Register. Rather it is on account of the horrific and unprecedented nature of her end, the most calamitous peacetime loss of an Irish Sea passenger vessel which occurred during the entire one hundred and seventy years after the introduction of steam power.

It may be difficult for anyone under fifty-five years of age to realise the intensity of the shock and horror experienced by people in Ireland (and particularly in the North) when the full extent of the tragedy of that day, in January 1953, became known. People in Britain felt the impact too of course, particularly seamen and relatives of those lost, but for Ireland the foundering of the *Princess Victoria* had a special poignancy. For many reasons, including the relative sizes of the populations of the two islands, the number of Irish people having relatives and friends in the larger country and the close business connections, a far higher proportion of the population of Ireland, than of Britain, had crossed the Irish Sea. To the inhabitants of Dublin, Belfast, Cork and Derry the Railway and Coast Lines ships were a part of daily life. In the year 1953 each had its cross-channel berths almost in the city centre and, in the cases of Dublin

Courtesy Belfast Telegraph

The ro-ro vessel *Princess Victoria*, built by Dennys in 1946, and the subject of the worst disaster ever to happen to an Irish Sea passenger ship in peacetime, is shown here leaving Larne. Her life of only seven years was one of the shortest, though not the shortest, of all the railway and Coast Lines ships.

and Belfast, Dun Laoghaire and Larne were not far away. This was only partially paralleled in London, Manchester, Birmingham and elsewhere in Britain by the main line services of the railways. What English office worker, for example, was afforded the equivalent of the marine panorama that everyday met the eye of the Belfast commuter as he or she made their way between the city centre and the suburban rail terminus of Queen's Quay? There, lined up day after day, in good or bad weather, were the five vessels: Ardrossan cargo, Glasgow passenger, Heysham passenger, Heysham cargo and Liverpool passenger and, more often than not, there were others further down the river. How could even the most land-oriented and unobservant person not be aware of what an integral part of the social structure were the cross channel ships?

Rough crossings, particularly in winter, were a fact of life, and sometimes journeys could be protracted by fog or storm. That a modern and apparently well found ship, operating on the shortest of all the regular crossings between Ireland and Britain, to a daily schedule that had been virtually unchanged for half a century, could be lost by stress of weather, with almost its entire complement of passengers and crew, was unbelievable. Today, with the sinkings of the *Herald of Free Enterprise* and the *Estonia* fresh in our minds, we probably no longer have the capacity to be shocked by such an event as the foundering of the *Princess Victoria*, but in 1953 we were stunned.

I well remember the day of the tragedy. At the time I was living in Bangor, on the south-eastern shore of Belfast Lough and, on that Saturday in January, I had made a detour along the sea front on my way home from work (we worked on Saturday mornings in those days), in order to drop off a colleague near her home. The weather was atrocious. I had to make a conscious effort to open the car door against the fierce south-east wind and, even within sheltered Bangor Bay, the spume and spindrift were being whipped from the tops of the sizeable waves.

Arriving home just before lunch time, I switched on the one o'clock radio news from which I heard that a ship, no name given, on the Stranraer-Larne service was in difficulties. Initially I, and no doubt many other listeners, felt no great cause for alarm. Certainly crew and passengers out there in the storm would be having a hard time but, unless there had been a breakdown of both main engines, fracture of both shafts, or loss of both propellers (unbelievable coincidences), eventually the vessel would turn up in one or other of her terminal ports.

As the afternoon wore on, however, the radio reports became increasingly ominous. The ship, now identified as the *Princess Victoria*, working the regular morning service ex Stranraer, was almost completely disabled. One of her lifeboats had been lowered and had got away. The Donaghadee lifeboat was at sea and other craft, both naval and civilian, were moving towards the reported position of the casualty. The three vessels nearest to *Princess Victoria*, when she broadcast her distress message, were the Burns and Laird Lines' *Lairdsmoor* (a modern cargo/livestock motor ship) on passage from Dublin to Glasgow with cattle and general cargo, one of William Sloan's elderly steamships (from memory the *Beauly*) on the Glasgow-Belfast-Bristol Channel service — both of which had been sheltering in Belfast Lough — and the small Glasgow registered coastal tanker *Pass of Drumochter*. Despite their operating to a concerted search plan agreed between their masters, none of these three vessels found the casualty, but the tanker did locate the railway vessel's lifeboat and was thus instrumental in ensuring that its pitifully small all-male complement were brought into Donaghadee, by that port's lifeboat under coxswain Nelson who, as soon as the rescued people had been landed, put to sea again.

Throughout the late afternoon and evening, and on into the winter night, we listened to the successive bulletins, expecting each time to hear that some of the ship's lifeboats had reached land or that people had been rescued from them by the searching vessels. It was not to be. Next morning, by which time the storm had passed and we woke to a grey but calm winter day, we learned that the *Princess Victoria* had sunk with the loss of her entire complement, bar a couple of crew members and a very few male passengers.

In due course came the official enquiry, whose findings were in brief that, shortly after leaving Loch Ryan, *Princess Victoria* had shipped a large amount of water, owing to the sea having broken open the half height stern doors, damaging them so that they could not be properly closed again. The wash ports were unable to rid the vessel of the mass of water which in any case was being

Courtesy Belfast Telegraph
Some of the tragically few survivors of the sinking of the *Princess Victoria*, after being brought to land by the Donaghadee lifeboat.

continually augmented through the damaged doors, so that the water being free to surge around the vehicle deck produced an ever increasing list which eventually doomed the vessel.

It seems that Captain Ferguson had considered returning to Loch Ryan but that an attempt to do so had to be abandoned, after it was found to be impossible to put the bow rudder into operation, owing to the danger to the lives of the crew members sent to the forecastle head to carry out this action. Presumably the need for the bow rudder arose because the ship was pitching so severely, constantly bringing the main rudder clear of the water, that without steering control at each end of the vessel it would have been hazardous to make the 180 degree turn necessary to bring *Princess Victoria* on course for Loch Ryan. So there was nothing left for the ship but to continue moving towards Ireland as best she might and under the best control that the master, his deck and engineer officers and other crew members, could continue to exercise.

It has been stated that shortly before the battered vessel's final moments, a garbled radio message (and that Operator David Broadbent continued transmitting with the ship almost on her beam ends is surely to his everlasting credit) came through to the effect that the Copeland lighthouse close to the southern entrance to Belfast Lough had been sighted. It was later established that this was almost certainly a misidentification of the light at Black Head, some miles north of the Copeland, at the opposite side of the Lough. If this misapprehension was the case, it may have been a factor in the heavy loss of life, in that the searching vessels, including the Donaghadee lifeboat, might otherwise have found the *Princess Victoria* before she went under.

However, it is open to doubt if many lives could have been saved. The heavy list and the appalling weather might well have precluded the successful launching of any boats, other than the one that got away some time before *Princess Victoria* sank. Even had more boats become waterborne, it would have been an almost impossible task to have got any but the most agile passengers (virtually all of whom would have been prostrated by seasickness and its consequent dehydration) up from below to the boat deck, and across the wet and almost vertical surface of the latter to the boats. In this connection we may note that the few passengers who did get into the ship's lifeboat, and were rescued, had been in the bar on the boat deck ever since leaving Stranraer. The ship's master obviously considered that there was a better chance of survival for all on board if they remained in the 'Princess' until, hopefully, she reached Larne (or possibly Belfast Lough). This might have seemed a better option than to attempt to get them into such boats as might have been launched, but which could well have been unmanageable in the storm, and in which people in their already weakened state could have succumbed to exposure.

At the very end a few people must have got away on life rafts as there were reports of some being sighted on one of these appliances but, although rafts were found on the day after the sinking, there were no survivors from them.

LATER STRANRAER-LARNE SHIPS

British Railways were in no hurry to replace the *Princess Victoria*. For the next eight years the ageing *Princess Margaret* continued her six days per week, all the year round, double crossings except when she was withdrawn for annual survey, when *Princess Maud* came north from Holyhead to be based again at her old home port, at which she continued to be registered. However, despite the lack of a permanent replacement for the lost vessel, the second daily summer service continued to operate by courtesy of the Southern Region of British Railways, from whom their Scottish colleagues were able to borrow the train ferry vessel, *Hampton Ferry*, 2989 grt, 360'x 62'2", one of the three twin-screw geared turbine 16½ knot ships built in 1934 to inaugurate the Dover-Dunkirk train ferry service.

The *Hampton Ferry*, with her side by side twin funnels and slab sided profile, brought a new look to the short sea route but no one could say that this immigrant from the south coast was an ideal replacement for the *Princess Victoria*. Noticeably slower than her predecessor, she was sadly deficient in public rooms and other normal amenities for daylight crossings. I made two passages in this vessel and, apart from my interest in travelling in a type of ship which was new to me, the only feature which remains in my memory, after more than thirty years (for the *Hampton Ferry* outlasted the *Princess Margaret*) is the excellence of the coffee. Presumably the catering staff were well versed in satisfying the exacting culinary demands of the French and Belgian members of their regular clientele. Had my experiences of the stop-gap vessel been as an inmate of a first class Wagons Lits sleeper proceeding to Paris or Brussels by 'Night Ferry', I might now remember her more kindly, but maybe not. What experience of the ship could I have gained from the inside of a railway coach? And so the *Hampton Ferry* is recollected as a source of fine coffee, from whose open stern on a peaceful summer evening one contemplated the calm sea against a background of the Galloway hills, whilst all the while remembering the tragedy that had been played out on that same sea just a few short years before.

Traffic on the Stranraer-Larne route declined during the 1950s and, towards the end of the decade, British Rail announced that it was considering abandoning Larne and running the service to and from Belfast. However, before this drastic step was taken, it was decided to make a final effort to boost traffic through Larne by providing a new purpose-built ro-ro vessel for the regular year round service. This ship, the turbine-engined *Caledonian Princess*, 3630 grt, 353' x 57'2", took up her duties in 1962 and brought about an immediate transformation in the flagging fortunes of the short sea route. Over the next thirty-five years it increased in popularity to the extent that it became the busiest of all the Irish Sea freight/passenger routes, despite strong competition from the P and O operation between Larne and Cairnryan, nearer to the mouth of Loch Ryan than Stranraer. In 1995, British Rails' earlier proposal to move the Stranraer Service from Larne to Belfast was implemented by the current operators, Stena Line.

The *Hampton Ferry* ceased to operate on the Larne-Stranraer route after 1966 and in her place Sealink (the new name for British Rail's shipping services) chartered the ro-ro ship *Stena Nordica* from the Swedish Stena Line. This vessel, which had been built in France in 1965 by Ateliers et Chantiers de la Seine Maritime at Le Trait, was of 2607 grt and had main dimensions of 261'10" x 53'2". Although few could have foreseen it at the time, this charter was a strangely prophetic action since, eventually, after various vicissitudes which need not concern us here, Stena – by then a multi-national concern – became the owners and operators of the erstwhile BR routes. Before this, however, Sealink BR had chartered a second ship – *Stena Normandica*, 5443 grt, 120.78m x 19.51m, built in 1974 for the Rosslare route. The ship was subsequently purchased by Sealink and became the *Saint Brendan*.

I made one trip in *Stena Nordica*, of which my abiding memory is that it provided my introduction to the more spartan and utilitarian standards of the new generation of cross-channel ship, soon to become universal but which, in the summer of 1967, compared unfavourably with what I had been accustomed to.

The year 1967 was an important one for the Stranraer-Larne service with the introduction of the twin-screw diesel engined *Antrim Princess*. This was the first British Rail/Sealink car ferry to have bow as well as stern doors, which greatly reduced the time taken to disembark vehicles. *Antrim Princess*, 3630 grt, 112.47m x 17.37m, was built by the Tyneside firm of Hawthorn Leslie and had a service speed of 19 knots.

Antrim Princess was followed by the generally similar *Ailsa Princess* in 1971. This ship had the same overall dimensions, but a slightly larger gross tonnage, 3715. However, unlike her elder sister, she was built in Italy. I never travelled in this latter vessel but a crossing from Larne in *Antrim Princess*, followed by a night on board prior to taking the early morning train to Glasgow, demonstrated that the old bugbear of the nocturnal cargo workings still persisted. Throughout the night there were sporadic activities on the vehicle deck, immediately above the sleeping accommodation.

The advent of the *Ailsa Princess*, together with the introduction of two basically freight vehicle carriers, *Ulidia* and *Darnia* (which however had some passenger accommodation), enabled *Caledonian Princess* to be withdrawn from the Larne-Stranraer service. After some alterations to her passenger accommodation, the ship was put into service on the Portsmouth-Channel Islands route, but subsequently became a general reserve and relief vessel. For example, I crossed in her from Holyhead to Dun Laoghaire during one Christmas holiday period in the 1970s. However, as a steam-powered ship the *Caledonian Princess* was uneconomic to operate compared to her newer diesel-engined sisters and was withdrawn, and scrapped, in the early 1980s, although mechanically and structurally good for at least another ten years' service.

Before taking leave of Larne, I think that a very brief mention should be made of two shipping companies which played a major role in the post-war development of that port, even though neither concern was connected with either Coast Lines or British Rail (though one of them was eventually acquired by the British Transport Commission). These companies were the incongruously named Atlantic Steam Navigation Company and Townsend Thoresen.

THE ATLANTIC STEAM NAVIGATION COMPANY

The ASN Co was established by Major Frank Bustard immediately after the Second World War. Major Bustard had been passenger manager of the former White Star Line, which was no doubt the reason for both the title of the new firm, and the naming policy for its ships. The official title of the White Star Line had been The Oceanic Steam Navigation Company, whilst the ships of the firm were given names ending in '...ic' (eg *Britannic*, *Titanic*). ASN vessels were given '...ic' names, followed by the word Ferry.

The new company set up a ro-ro service for freight vehicles and their drivers between Preston and Larne in 1946, using former tank landing ships bought from the British government. Later, the operation was extended to include Belfast, and in due course a totally new route between Tilbury and Rotterdam was established. The Atlantic Steam Navigation Company was taken over by the British Transport Commission (not, be it noted, by British Rail) in 1954. Soon after the change of ownership, the replacement of the former tank landing ships with purpose built vessels began, the first new ships being the *Bardic Ferry* and *Ionic Ferry*. The main details of the *Ionic Ferry*, which may serve as a typical example of the company's purpose built vessels, were that it was built by Dennys in 1958, was of 2438 grt, and had main dimensions 103.62m x 16.82m.

The profile of the new ships was unconventional in that the accommodation for crew and passengers, (mostly though not exclusively lorry drivers) was right up in the fore part of the ship, leaving a long clear open space above the enclosed vehicle deck. The impression given was that of an overgrown oil rig supply vessel. In the history of Irish Sea freight services, the Atlantic Steam Navigation Company, the pioneers of regular ro-ro operations, will always hold a prominent position.

TOWNSEND THORESEN

The establishment of the firm of Townsend Thoresen was a joint venture between the Norwegian Thoresen concern and the English company Townsend Brothers, who had set up a Dover-Calais service specifically for motorists and their cars in the 1930s. This, however, was not a ro-ro operation.

Townsend Thoresen introduced purpose built ro-ro vessels to the English Channel in the early post-war years and subsequently established a route between Larne and Cairnryan at the mouth of Loch Ryan, appreciably nearer to Larne than Stranraer at the head of the Loch. Cairnryan had been built (if that is the correct word) as a reserve port in case of serious air raid or other damage to Glasgow, or its narrow approaches up the River Clyde. Fortunately, Cairnryan never had to serve the basic purpose for which it had been established, but it was nevertheless kept in being after the end of the war. Had this port not been available for Townsend Thoresen, it is unlikely that their service could have been set up. Stranraer, as well as being limited in size and as regards facilities, was railway owned and hence was unlikely to have been made available by BR to a competitor.

The Larne-Cairnryan service was for both private and commercial vehicles, and their drivers and passengers, and at the start was operated by Viking vessels. These ships, of a general type which was used by several Scandinavian companies in the 1960s and 1970s, had a squat appearance, emphasised by their rather small thin funnels, placed one at each side of the extreme breadth of the ship. Another factor which contributed to the squat profile was the proportion of beam (breadth) to the the ship's length, approximately 1:5.6. This was not an unduly high figure for a ro-ro vessel, but noticeably higher than figures of around 1:7 for the conventional vessels to which, in the 1960s, one was accustomed. Later, as Townsend Thoresen introduced larger vessels, of newer designs, to the English Channel, examples of these latter types appeared at Larne also. As representative of the Vikings we may cite *Viking Two*, 3670 grt, 99.49m x 17.1m, built by Koldnes, Tonsberg in 1964. This particular ship was later acquired by Sealink who renamed it *Earl William* and used her primarily on the Weymouth-Channel Islands service. However, this vessel did reach the Irish Sea, even if only for a short period, and an account of a crossing I made in her in 1988 will be found later in the book.

It is likely that the name Townsend Thoresen will be remembered in shipping circles for a long time, on account of the loss in March 1987 of that company's *Herald of Free Enterprise*, shortly after she had left Zeebrugge for Dover with her bow doors open. In the scathing report of the Court of Enquiry, the underlying reason for the disaster was given as the slackness which permeated all levels of the company, from senior management downwards. Shortly after the loss of the *Herald of Free Enterprise*, Townsend Thoresen went out of business, and its ships and routes were taken over by P and O. Under the auspices of this company the Larne-Cairnryan service has continued to prosper and, with the recent move of Sealink's former Larne operations to Belfast, it is now the major passenger service in and out of Larne.

HEYSHAM AND FLEETWOOD TO BELFAST

Despite their common ownership from 1923 onwards, the services to Belfast from the neighbouring ports of Heysham and Fleetwood continued their separate existences until 1928. During those five years the Heysham route was served by the former Midland Railway sister ships, *Antrim*, 1954 grt and *Londonderry*, 1968 grt, each of which had been built in 1904 with dimensions of 330'x 42' and with twin reciprocating engines, and by the ex Lancashire and Yorkshire/LNWR *Duke of Cornwall*, 1528 grt, 315' x 37', which had similar machinery, but was six years older than the two Midland ships. There was also another, smaller, ex Midland Railway vessel at Heysham in the early 1920s, the *Duchess of Devonshire* which, however, seems to have operated more often to the Isle of Man than to Ireland.

The three elderly vessels, just mentioned, maintained a nightly service to and from Belfast carrying passengers and general cargo, of which rail-parcels were an important component. At Heysham, which had been established as a cross channel port by the Midland Railway in 1904, there was direct railway communication at the quayside to and from London and other British centres. Donegall Quay, Belfast, within easy reach of the city centre, was rail connected for freight traffic, but passengers had to use taxis or walk to and from the city's three railway termini. Passenger facilities at the quayside were nil, as they remained for the duration of 'conventional' services to Heysham. Heysham at least had railway platforms, but at Belfast one walked across the railway goods lines, threaded one's way through the mass of disgorging taxis and the cargo transit shed and up the gangway. A ticket check at the entrance to this appliance was an unappreciated prelude to embarkation, particularly on a wet winter night with a chill wind blowing through the draughty shed. The transit of the railway tracks, where shunting operations might be in progress, was not an antic to be recommended to the elderly, or to those with small children. There were porters available to put luggage on board but my main recollection of them is of their standing round the purser's bureau in the scrum of passengers whose minds were fixed on claiming their sleeping berths, or on the chance of obtaining one at the last moment, whilst the mental concentration of the porters was directed towards ensuring that no passenger got away without bestowing the obligatory (if unofficial) tip.

During the last five years of its existence, the Fleetwood-Belfast service which, as regards times of operation, railway connections and general facilities, was very similar to the Heysham one, was maintained by three ex LYR/LNWR ships, *Duke of Connaught*, *Duke of Cumberland* and *Duke of Argyll*. The first named was of 1564 grt with main dimensions of 315'x 38', was propelled by twin screw reciprocating engines and had been built in 1902. The *Duke of Cumberland* and the *Duke of Argyll* were sister ships of 2036 and 2039 grt respectively and with dimensions of 330'x 41' in each case. These vessels, which had been built in 1909, had triple screws with direct drive turbine machinery.

The Fleetwood service was closed down in 1928 and the *Dukes of Argyll* and

 (Continued on page 30)

IRISH SEA ROUTES 1939

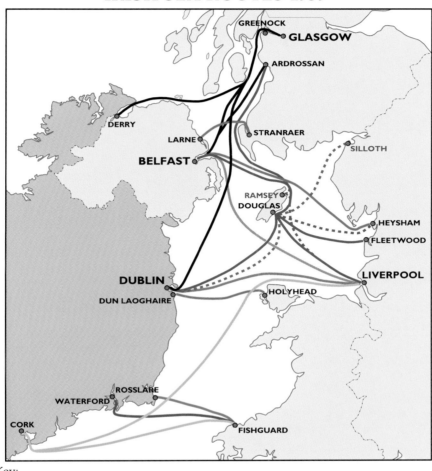

Key:

London, Midland and Scottish Railway } British Railways after 1948
Great Western Railway
Fishguard and Rosslare Railways and Harbours Company
(operated by the GWR, later British Railways.)
Belfast Steamship Company
British and Irish Steam Packet Company
Burns and Laird Lines (Belfast-Ardrossan operated in the summer only)
Isle of Man Steam Packet Company (Douglas-Liverpool all the year round. Other routes May-September only)
City of Cork Steam Packet Company (merged with B and I in 1936)
Dublin and Silloth Steamship Company

(Services with broken lines were discontinued after World War II.)

Brian Boyle

The twin screw turbine vessel *Caledonian Princess*, delivered by Dennys to British Rail in 1962, leaving Larne for Stranraer. The stern door is in process of being closed. It is no exaggeration to say that this 3630 grt ship saved the Larne-Stranraer route from closure in the early 1960s.

Derek Young

Stena Nordica, 2607 grt, built in France in 1965, pictured at Larne in August 1967. This Stena Line ship had been chartered by Sealink in the previous year to operate on the Larne-Stranraer service pending the building of *Ailsa Princess*. Note the large dummy funnel, typical of many 'Viking' type ro-ros.

Barry Carse

Duke of Rothesay, built in 1956, arriving at the ro-ro berth at Carlisle Pier, Dun Laoghaire on 3rd August 1974. Note that the ship, which was converted to a side loading ro-ro vessel in 1967, now has stern loading facilities in this view.

Barry Carse

The steamship *Avalon* was originally built in 1963 for the British Rail's Harwich-Hook of Holland service, and for the operation of cruises to European ports. She was subsequently converted for ro-ro service, and ran first on the Fishguard-Rosslare and subsequently the Holyhead-Dun Laoghaire routes. The picture shows her at Carlisle Pier, Dun Laoghaire in December 1975. This view shows the now lifted harbour branch of the railway.

Brian Boyle

The MS *Ionic Ferry*, 2438 grt, built by Dennys in 1958, was one of the first two purpose built ro-ro vessels for the Atlantic Steam Navigation Company's services between Preston and Larne/Belfast. These services were mainly for commercial vehicles .

Barry Carse

Innisfallen, 4849 grt, built by Verolme Cork Dockyard in 1969 as the *Leinster*, for the B and I S P Co's Dublin-Liverpool service. As *Innisfallen* she was set to work on the B and I's Cork-Swansea route. By the time this photo was taken the route was Rosslare-Pembroke. *Innisfallen*, ex *Leinster* is shown here approaching Rosslare in August 1984.

Barry Carse

The British and Irish Steam Packet Company's *Connacht*, 6812 grt, built by Verolme Cork Dockyard in 1979, alongside the North Wall Extension, Dublin. The ship is in her original style of painting. In 1988 the *Connacht* was sold to Brittany Ferries and renamed *Duchesse Anne*.

J McGregor's collection

The twin-screw steamship *Antrim*, one of the pioneer vessels of the former Midland railway route between Heysham and Belfast. The *Antrim*, which had been built in 1904, was 1954 gross tons and had main dimensions of 330'x 42'. The picture shows the ship with its original MR funnel markings. She was later sold to the Isle of Man Steam Packet Company where she became the *Ramsey Town*.

Vickers Ltd

The *Duke of Cornwall*, 1528 grt, 315'x 37', was built in 1898 for the Fleetwood-Belfast service jointly operated by the Lancashire and Yorkshire and London North Western Railway companies. This vessel was transferred to the Heysham service after the formation of the LMS in 1923. In 1928 it was sold to the IOMSP Co who renamed it *Rushen Castle*.

Cumberland, together with the *Londonderry* from Heysham were transferred to the newly established route between Tilbury and Dunkirk. This was an Anglo-French venture, whose operating organisation was the Angleterre, Lorraine Alsace Steamship Company, with which the LMS was closely involved. The three vessels just-mentioned were renamed *Alsacien, Picard* and *Flamand* respectively. Also in 1928, the *Antrim* and the *Duke of Cornwall* were sold to the Isle of Man Steam Packet Company, under whose ownership they became the *Ramsey Town* and the *Rushen Castle.* The former was scrapped in 1936 but *Rushen Castle* lasted for a further ten years. I remember seeing her working on the Dublin-Douglas summer only service in 1933.

To revert for a moment to the Tilbury-Dunkirk service, this provided an attractive route for passengers from south Yorkshire and the English Midlands to and from France and Belgium, via Saint Pancras station, London. During some summers of the late 1920s and the 1930s connections from Belfast to France, via Dunkirk were advertised, including the provision of a through carriage from Stranraer to Saint Pancras, connecting from the morning sailing ex-Larne.

From 1928 onwards, railway steamer services from and to Belfast were concentrated on Heysham and, to maintain these, Dennys delivered three new 'Dukes' in that year. These vessels were the *Duke of Argyll, Duke of Lancaster* and *Duke of Rothesay,* twin-screw, twenty-one knot, geared-turbine ships with main dimensions of 360' x 53' and gross tonnages of 3799, 3794 and 3805 respectively. Shortly before the newcomers took up service, the main rail connection between Heysham and London was changed from the former Midland route via Leeds to the ex-LNWR main line via Crewe, which produced an appreciable saving of time. As a result of this alteration the London departure/arrival station for the Heysham boat trains became Euston, in place of Saint Pancras.

The new 'Dukes' made the overnight crossing in about seven hours. Berthing at Heysham, at around 0530, was not universally popular with passengers, but the connecting train services ensured early arrivals in London, Leeds, Manchester and elsewhere. The late evening departure from Belfast was also advantageous for some passengers. In the opposite direction a late afternoon/early evening train from London ensured an arrival in Belfast at around 0630 the following morning. During the summer and at other busy periods, occasional daylight services were operated. I crossed only once from Belfast to Heysham by day, in the summer of 1961. My main recollection of this journey is of the impressive views of the extreme south west of Scotland, the Isle of Man and the mountains of the English Lake District.

As befitted their normal schedules, the new ships had rather limited lounge and bar accommodation but a generous provision of cabin and other sleeping facilities. They had a large amount of space for cargo which was loaded and discharged on the port sides by shore based gear. There was little, if any, accommodation for livestock on the new 'Dukes'. My memory is not too accurate here, but certainly I never saw cattle being loaded on to any of them. Four legged travellers were, however, catered for in the *Duke of Abercorn* and

World Ship Society

The twin-screw turbine vessel *Duke of Lancaster*, built by Dennys in 1928 for the LMSR's Heysham-Belfast route. This ship was of 3794 gross tons and had main dimensions of 360'8"x 53'. Note the black lifeboats, a somewhat unusual feature for a cross-channel passenger vessel.

Duke of York, shortly to be described and, from 1936, in the new *Slieve Bearnagh* which had no passenger accommodation.

In outward appearance the *Dukes of Lancaster*, *Argyll* and *Rothesay* were typical of their period, with two funnels, two-deck-high superstructures (of which the lower was plated in but the upper had open side decks), and cruiser sterns. Three boats per side were carried amidships and one aft. Although I first travelled by the Heysham route in 1937, it was not until the late 1940s and the 1950s that I came to know the 1928 'Dukes' at all well. At this latter time, unusually, the lifeboats were painted black. Whether in earlier days they had been the almost universal white, I cannot remember. All but one of my passages in these ships were in the saloon accommodation and my one experience of their steerage is remembered as being as unattractive as any other I had at the after end of any inter-war railway ship.

It might be thought that the three new vessels would have been adequate to maintain the Heysham-Belfast service, particularly since in an emergency a Stranraer or Holyhead based ship could probably have been called on. However, in 1930 the twin-screw turbine-engined *Curraghmore*, 1587 grt, 307'x 40', which had been built in 1919 for the Holyhead-Greenore service, was renamed *Duke of Abercorn*. It was given some extra passenger accommodation, which increased the gross tonnage to 2217, and transferred to Heysham. From Heysham the *Duke of Abercorn* ran to and from Belfast, mainly as a cargo/livestock vessel, but carrying passengers during peak periods and emergencies. However the erstwhile *Curraghmore*, appreciably smaller than her running mates, did not remain long on the Heysham-Belfast route. Traffic was increasing and, in 1935, a fourth new ship, the *Duke of York*, 3743 grt, 329'x 52', was delivered to the LMS by Harland and Wolff. It seems likely that Harlands, rather than the faithful Dennys, were chosen as builders owing to financial assistance being made available to the Belfast firm by the Government of Northern Ireland. As had been the case with the *Duke of Abercorn* (now disposed of), the *Duke of York* operated cargo/livestock or passenger services, as required. Twenty feet shorter than the other 'Dukes', the new vessel, like them, was powered by geared-turbines driving twin-screws, and was coal-fired.

During the Second World War, the *Duke of York* ran for a while on the route for which the ship had been built (I crossed in the vessel from Heysham early in 1942), but was also directly involved in war service and, as a Landing Ship, took part in the invasion of Normandy. At that time, a striking painting of the *Duke of York* and the *Princess Maud*, off the Normandy coast, was a major decorative feature in one of the 1956 'Dukes' – from memory the *Duke of Lancaster*. In 1948, very soon after the LMS became part of British Railways, the *Duke of York* was moved to Harwich to work on the former London and North Eastern Railway's Hook of Holland service. The ship was converted to oil firing in 1950 and, at the same time, given additional passenger accommodation and lost one of her funnels. She reappeared briefly on the Irish Sea in 1951, replacing the *Princess Maud* at Holyhead when the latter went to Southampton for the summer service to and from Saint Malo. The *Duke of York* was seriously damaged in a collision off Harwich in 1953 but, after having a new bow fitted, she returned to her adopted home port, from which she continued to operate until the 1960s.

The three 1928 'Dukes' all survived the war, during which they were variously employed, including putting in some service on their peacetime route. They returned permanently to Heysham and Belfast and continued to run between these two ports until 1956, when they were replaced by three new turbine vessels bearing the same names. These 1928 ships were steady dependable craft, which served their owners well, but I have always considered them to have been the least interesting of all the passenger ships which ran on the Irish Sea routes during the inter-war years.

As was the case with the Stranraer-Larne route, the Heysham-Belfast route was served by several 'foreign' vessels at various times during the Second World War, although these were largely replacing the 'Dukes' on the regular sailings. Heysham did not see anything like the great amount of military and naval passenger traffic which was the reason for the appearance of so many 'strangers' on extra services at Stranraer. So far as I am aware, the two 'outside' passenger ships, which put in the greatest amount of time between Heysham and Belfast during the war years, were the *Cambria*, one of the three express mail vessels on the Holyhead-Dun Laoghaire service, and the *Louth* of the British and Irish Steam Packet Company, an elderly ship which had had a varied career under two different nominal owners. Both of these vessels will be more fully referred to later in this narrative.

I know of only one passenger vessel other than the four 'Dukes', the *Cambria*, the *Louth* (and possibly, in the very early war years, the *Princess Margaret*) having run on the Heysham-Belfast passenger service during the war. This was the *Dewsbury*, 1686 grt, 265'x 36', an LNER ship, built in 1910 and originally one of the former Great Central Railway's fleet, based at Immingham on the Humber estuary, which appeared on the route in the autumn of 1939. It is a not unreasonable assumption that one or more of the regular vessels were at that time transporting troops to France. There may of course have been other temporary additions to the Heysham fleet.

By the year 1955, the 1928 'Dukes' were twenty-seven years old. They had worked hard all their lives and were due for renewal. Despite the misgivings about the future of the Larne service, which British Railways were starting to voice at about that time, the organisation obviously still saw a prosperous future for the Heysham route. Three new *Dukes of Argyll, Lancaster* and *Rothesay*, to have considerably higher standards of passenger comfort and general amenities, were ordered, and delivered in 1956 — two by Harland and Wolff and one, the *Duke of Rothesay*, by Dennys. These were 21 knot twin-screw steamships with gross tonnages of 4797 for the *Duke of Argyll* and *Duke of Lancaster* and 4780 for the *Duke of Rothesay*. Overall main dimensions were 376'1"x 57'4". Despite the fact that the two ships delivered by Harlands in 1949 for the railway service between Holyhead and Dun Laoghaire (of almost the same size and having similar maximum service speeds) were diesel powered, and notwithstanding their builders' long experience and acknowledged expertise as constructors of marine diesel engines, the new 'Dukes' were powered by the conventional and well tried geared turbines. This may well soon have been regretted by BR, as fuel prices increased sharply at about the time the ships took up service and continued to rise sporadically for a number of years.

The new Heysham vessels were of the three island type, having short raised forecastles, long midship structures and short poops. In contrast to their earlier namesakes these were single funnelled vessels, both of whose masts, which were of the tripod type, rose directly from the midship structure and not from the fore and after well decks. Third class accommodation was of a distinctly higher standard than that of the earlier 'Dukes' and, a notable advance, was all contained within the midship structure. No longer did 'steerage' bear witness to its title by its proximity to the rudder. The lower deck of the midship structure was extended to the full beam of the ship and contained sleeping accommodation and a first class lounge. Above this were the first class 'restaurant' and the third class 'cafeteria' — thus were Victorian social distinctions preserved in the titles of twentieth century catering facilities, the galley, the entrance halls/bureaux for each class, the saloon bar and the third class lounge. Both the restaurant and the cafeteria were attractively situated, with wide windows looking out onto glassed-in promenade decks. Above, on the boat deck, with its five boats per side carried in gravity davits, were more saloon sleeping accommodation, and engineer officers' accommodation. Finally, on what was designated the 'lower deck', were more cabins for third class passengers and their bar accommodation.

Whilst the new ships provided greatly improved standards of accommodation for each class of passenger, and more especially for the 'thirds', they had one noticeable fault — vibration — a particularly unwelcome feature in vessels designed to operate at night and which purported to offer comfortable sleeping facilities to their clients. A degree of vibration had come to be accepted as the norm in motor ships but in brand new, state of the art, turbine vessels it was as unexpected as it was unwelcome. Just what caused the trouble I do not know, but it must have been a fault in the basic design, as it was apparent in all three ships. That it was as apparent to British Railways management, as it was to ordinary travellers, is evidenced by the fact that once, when I mentioned this trouble to a senior railway official who frequently travelled between London and Belfast, he made no attempt to deny the existence of the fault. I do not know if any steps were ever taken to try and remedy the matter; certainly I never made a passage in any of the three 'Dukes' without experiencing this persistent vibration. However, to speak fairly, it was scarcely of motor ship proportions.

No doubt, when the decision was taken to build the new vessels, it was presumed that they would have the normal twenty-five to thirty year economic life of their predecessors and other former railway owned steamships. However, the importance of two factors in the mid 1950s was greatly underestimated, if indeed they were recognised at all. During the following decade, they led to a decline in passenger traffic on the Heysham route and to the premature withdrawal of the post-war *Dukes of Argyll, Lancaster* and *Rothesay*. These first of these factors was the great and continuing increase in cross-channel air travel, thanks to the introduction of turbo prop and, soon afterwards, fully jet propelled aircraft. Second, coincidentally with the growth of private car ownership and of road freight services, there was the development of ro-ro services, which were largely concentrated on the shortest sea crossings. So far as the Heysham route was concerned this latter factor ensured that Heysham's loss became Stranraer's gain.

The withdrawal of the 'Dukes' took place gradually. The first sign of change was the conversion of the *Duke of Rothesay* from a conventional passenger/cargo vessel to a side-loading ro-ro vessel in 1967, which was done in order to provide a replacement for the thirty-five year old *Saint Andrew* on the Fishguard-Rosslare route. I will have more to say about this altered 'Duke' when we come to deal with the activities of the Fishguard and Rosslare Railways and Harbours Company. Meanwhile, all that need be said here is that as long as the Belfast-Heysham service continued to operate, the *Duke of Rothesay* made occasional reappearances on it as a relief vessel.

For a while after their sister ship (can a 'Duke' be a sister?) took itself off to Wales and the south east of Ireland, the *Duke of Argyll* and the *Duke of Lancaster* continued their regular nightly crossings but it was not long before they too underwent conversion to cater for ro-ro traffic, though with stern loading. These two ships did not last long in their new role, however. In 1974 they were withdrawn and the Belfast-Heysham passenger service ceased to operate. Ro-ro freight facilities, using chartered vessels, continued to be provided for some time but in the long run these too became uncompetitive, vis à vis the attractions of Stranraer. Today, the Heysham-Belfast connection is but one of the many Irish Sea memories of the middle-aged and older generations of travellers.

The *Duke of Argyll* and the *Duke of Lancaster*, each of which put in brief appearances on the Holyhead-Dun Laoghaire route in their last years, were sold in 1975, the former going to a Cyprus company, under whose ownership (and renamed *Neptunia*), she operated between Ancona and Haifa, with calls at Corfu, Piraeus and Rhodes. She was still in Lloyds' Register in 1985. The *Duke of Lancaster*, which was bought by the Liverpool firm of Empire Wise, became an accommodation ship, lying beached on the Welsh shore of the Dee estuary, where I saw her several times when travelling by rail from and to Holyhead in the later 1970s. My last sight of this relatively short-lived vessel was in 1987 when, in the course of a visit to friends living on the Wirral Peninsula, I was at Parkgate, a little settlement on the opposite side of the Dee Estuary to the *Duke of Lancaster*'s resting place and from where, in the far distance, I descried this once elegant ship. Perhaps it was appropriate that I should see this last survivor of so many generations of conventional Irish Sea passenger ships from Parkgate, at one time a regular port of departure from Britain to Ireland but now, like the *Duke of Lancaster*, merely a relic of former glories. The *Duke of Rothesay* was withdrawn from the Fishguard-Rosslare route in 1971. Over the next four years she made some appearances on the Holyhead-Dun Laoghaire service and also on the Heysham-Belfast route. However, for much of this time she was laid up. She was withdrawn and scrapped in 1975, just nineteen years old.

LIVERPOOL-DROGHEDA

The Lancashire and Yorkshire Railway Company's service between Liverpool and Drogheda, which had been acquired from a private Drogheda-based firm well before the First World War, was a secondary one so far as the conveyance of passengers was concerned, though it was important for general cargo and particularly for the carriage of livestock from Ireland. In 1920 the vessels employed on the route were the *Mellifont* and the *Colleen Bawn*, twin-screw reciprocating engined steamships of 1088 and 1085 gross tons respectively, and with main dimensions of 260' x 35' in each case. *Colleen Bawn* had been built in 1903 and *Mellifont* in 1908.

Under the ownership of the LMS railway, the two ships continued to ply between Liverpool and Drogheda until 1928, in which year the service was taken over by the Coast Lines combine, with the British and Irish Steam Packet

Company (the B and I Line) as operators. So far as I know the B and I never carried passengers from or to Drogheda, although they continued to run the freight service until the end of 'conventional' operations in the very early 1970s.

After the change of operators, the *Mellifont* and *Colleen Bawn* remained with the LMS but were transferred to Holyhead, from which port they worked on cargo and livestock services until they were withdrawn for scrapping, *Colleen Bawn* in 1931 and *Mellifont* two years later. Very occasionally, at times of peak traffic, *Mellifont* was used as an extra passenger carrier between Holyhead and Dun Laoghaire. I do not remember her sister ever being so employed. It is possible that one or both of these ships may have carried third class passengers between Holyhead and Dublin (North Wall) during their final few years.

HOLYHEAD-GREENORE

As the Holyhead to Greenore route had its passenger service severely curtailed after 1926, there is not much to be said about it here. Somewhat surprisingly, in 1920 no fewer than five ships were available for what was, at best, a secondary service. These vessels were *Rostrevor* 805 grt, 272'x 35', built in 1895; *Galteemore* 1112 grt, 276'x 35', dating from 1898; *Rathmore*, 1569 grt, 299'x 40'8", built in 1908; *Greenore* 1488 grt, 306'x 40' of 1912 and *Curraghmore*, 1587 grt, 307'x 40', which had been delivered by Dennys in 1919. The *Curraghmore* was provided with geared-turbines driving twin-screws, whilst *Greenore*'s machinery was of the older triple-screw direct-drive turbine type. The other three ships had reciprocating engines. All five vessels were coal-fired.

The *Rostrevor*, *Galteemore* and *Greenore* were disposed of in the early 1920s, leaving *Curraghmore* and *Rathmore* to carry on the service during the last few years in which first class passengers were carried. No doubt the drastic reduction in the number of ships was due to the service having been cut down from a six to a three nights per week one, in each direction. It is interesting that the older reciprocating-engined *Rathmore* was retained as the standby vessel for the new *Curraghmore*, rather than the newer turbine-driven *Greenore*. Presumably, at the relatively modest speeds at which the Greenore route ships operated, the *Rathmore* was the more economical vessel. The metamorphosis of *Curraghmore* into *Duke of Abercorn* has already been noted. In 1927, *Rathmore* went to Tilbury to work on the ALAS Co route, to and from Dunkirk, under the name of *Lorrain*.

After 1926, cargo ships, some of which had third class passenger accommodation, ran three times weekly between Holyhead and Greenore. Brief details of these vessels are given in the next section. After the outbreak of the Second World War, the regular Greenore service was reduced to two, and later to one sailing each way per week though, during the duration of the conflict, there were special 'extras' from time to time. The route was closed completely in 1951. No passengers were carried during the war or subsequently.

No account of the Holyhead-Greenore service would be complete without a reference to the loss of the *Connemara*, which occurred in 1916, midway through the First World War, which presumably accounts for the tragedy having remained relatively unknown to the present day.

Briefly, what happened was that the *Connemara*, (built in 1897, 1106 grt, 272′5″x 35′1″), left Greenore on a winter evening of exceptionally severe weather and very soon afterwards collided with the Newry registered collier *Retriever* at the eastern end of the approach channel to Carlingford Lough. Both ships sank almost immediately and, out of the combined complements of the two vessels, eleven in the *Retriever* and sixty-seven (crew and passengers) in the *Connemara*, only one man, a member of the *Retriever* crew, survived. He succeeded in swimming to shore, a very considerable feat, not only on account of the weather conditions, but also because of the strong currents in and out of Carlingford Lough. A few cattle from the *Connemara* also reached land.

At the official enquiry it was stated that the *Retriever*'s navigation lights had been extinguished by the wind and sea and that it had not been possible to relight them on account of the appalling weather.

HOLYHEAD-DUBLIN (NORTH WALL)

During the inter-war years the passenger service on this route was provided by cargo/livestock vessels which had third class accommodation only. The frequency of the operation varied between one and two sailings per day in each direction, passage time being about 4 ½ hours. In 1919, the ships available for the North Wall service were *South Stack*, built 1900; *Snowdon*, built 1904; *Slieve Bawn*, built 1905; *Slieve Bloom*, built 1905 and *Slieve Gallion*, which dated from 1908. All five vessels had twin-screws, were long and low in profile, had average dimensions of 300′x 40′, gross tonnages varying between 1000 and 1100 and were capable of considerably higher speeds than those of contemporary Coast Lines cargo ships. In 1921, the final vessel of the type and the last reciprocating engined steamship to be built for the Irish Sea routes of the LNWR/LMS, the *Slieve Donard*, took up service at Holyhead. Her main dimensions were 310′x 39′, gross tonnage was 1116 and service speed 16 knots. The *Slieve Donard* may have been a cattle boat but, as was the case with her elder sisters, she had attractive lines, and indeed there was a certain grace about her: the long low hull, well raked masts and centrally placed funnel gave an impression of speed and efficiency uncommon with vessels of her type. The *Slieve Donard* lasted until 1953. How many crossings of the Irish Sea she made in her thirty-two years, I do not know but it was probably something in the neighbourhood of four thousand return trips. I doubt if she ever got to any ports other than Holyhead, Dublin or Greenore, unlike some of her younger running mates, of whom at least three had spells on the Heysham-Belfast service and one, and possibly more, had war service. *Slieve Donard*'s bell has been preserved and is displayed in the foyer of the Stena Line offices at Dun Laoghaire.

All of the older cargo vessels were disposed of in the 1930s, *South Stack* being the first to go. The final one was *Slieve Bawn* in 1935. I last saw her on a perfect windless summer evening in 1934. At about 1800 I was on the boat deck of Burns

E Kenny's collection

A typical Irish Sea collier, the *Glencree* owned by the Alliance and Dublin Consumers' Gas Company.

and Laird's *Lairdshill*, about to leave North Wall for Glasgow. Up the River Liffey, silent and graceful, glided *Slieve Bawn*, and eased into her berth astern of us, completely stealing the show from the colliers alongside the south bank of the river immediately opposite, and even from the younger and by no means ungainly *Lairdshill*.

The time expired cargo ships were replaced by four new twin-screw turbine vessels: *Slieve Bloom*, 310′x 44′6″, 1297 grt, in 1930; *Slieve More*, with the same overall dimensions but with a tonnage of 1408, in 1932; *Slieve League,* again with the same measurements but of 1342 grt, in 1935, and finally another *Slieve Bawn*, 310′x 45′, 1447 grt, in 1937. *Slieve Bloom* and *Slieve More* had the Holyhead cargo vessels' traditional speed of 16 knots. The two later ships were capable of an additional knot. Of this new quartet, only *Slieve More* had passenger accommodation, which of course was 'steerage' only.

As well as being larger and, in two cases, faster than their predecessors, the four ships of the 1930s had a very different appearance, with considerably greater beam and almost upright masts and funnels, together with free standing cranes on their flush decks. They had a completely utilitarian look, not ugly but altogether lacking the grace of *Slieve Donard* and her sisters. All accommodation, including the passenger facilities in *Slieve More*, was concentrated in a midship structure which rose just one deck above the otherwise completely flush profile. In *Slieve Bloom* and *Slieve More* this superstructure was carried out to the full width of the vessel, the two later ships having narrow side decks amidships. *Slieve Bloom*, whose bridge was merely the forward end of the top of the superstructure, had a particularly squat appearance.

HOLYHEAD-DUN LAOGHAIRE

In the years coming up to the outbreak of the First World War, the LNWR had four express steamers based on Holyhead, the *Cambria* (1897), *Anglia* (1900), *Hibernia* (1900) and *Scotia* (1902), sister ships of between 1842 and 1872 gross tonnage, on main dimensions of 329' / 330' x 39'. The vessels had triple expansion engines, with two low pressure cylinders per engine, driving twin screws. These four ships maintained a nightly express service between Dublin (North Wall) and Holyhead, carrying passengers and perishable cargo, together with railway parcels, and also a 'Daylight' express passenger service between Holyhead and Dun Laoghaire. There were direct main line rail connections at Holyhead and Dun Laoghaire and local connections between Dublin termini and North Wall, at which place the LNWR owned its own station and a hotel. It should be noted that, although the port (or rather the inner harbour) of Holyhead was owned by the LNWR, the Irish Mail steamers were neither owned nor operated by that company before 1919, but by the City of Dublin Steam Packet Company. The mail steamers used the 'Admiralty Pier' and not the inner quays at which the railway vessels berthed.

The *Cambria* and *Scotia* survived the war but the *Hibernia*, as HMS *Tara*, was lost in the Mediterranean and the *Anglia* too became a war casualty. Soon after the end of the conflict, the *Cambria* and *Scotia* were renamed *Arvonia* and *Menavia*. The former was scrapped about 1923 but, on the formation of the LMS in that year, the *Menavia* was transferred to Heysham to work on the former Midland Railway service to the Isle of Man. She was broken up in 1928, in which year the Isle of Man Steam Packet Company took over the Heysham-Douglas route. There is an exhibition model of the *Cambria* in the Irish National Maritime

Sean Kennedy/Green studios

One of the London and North Western Railway Company's Holyhead-based express passenger vessels built between 1897 and 1902.

Laurence Liddle

The farther building is the former LNWR Company's hotel at North Wall, Dublin. In LMS days this building housed that company's Irish head offices, the hotel having been closed after withdrawal of the North Wall-Holyhead express passenger service.

World Ship Society

The London, Midland and Scottish Railway Company's mail vessel *Scotia*, built in 1921 by Dennys of Dumbarton. The *Scotia*, which had a gross tonnage of 3450 and main dimensions of 381' x 45', was one of the two war losses of the LMS Co's Irish Sea fleet, the other being the 1939 *Princess Victoria*. The *Scotia* was lost at Dunkirk, together with many of her peacetime crew. This picture was taken before the 1932 refit.

Museum in Dun Laoghaire.

The express passenger service between Holyhead and Dublin (North Wall) was not continued after the First World War though, as we have seen, it remained possible to travel between these two ports in cargo ships with steerage accommodation only. In the 1920s and early 1930s the single fare by this latter service was seven shillings and sixpence (37½p). There was a major change in the Holyhead express services soon after the end of the war as the railway company had been awarded the mail contract, with the result that the City of Dublin Company's ships no longer came and went at Holyhead. It was generally believed in Ireland, that the LNWR had made good use of its political connections when tendering for the contract. I cannot say what truth, if any, there was in this belief but it seems not unlikely that the 'Premier Line' would have had, and used, influence in 'establishment' circles.

Anyway, influence or not, from 1920 until September 1939, at first the London and North Western, and later the London, Midland and Scottish, maintained a twice daily seven days per week express passenger and mail service on the Dun Laoghaire route. In the later 1920s, however, the daylight, though not the night, Sunday service was withdrawn. A result of this amendment to the timetable was that, apart from during the summer holiday season and at other peak periods, and despite the fact that after 1928 the railway companies and Coast Lines were between them operating no fewer than thirteen weekday cross channel services, the sole connection from Ireland to Britain on a Sunday was by the Dun Laoghaire-Holyhead night service. In the reverse direction one could travel on a Sunday evening/Monday morning via Stranraer as well as via Holyhead.

In those pre-airline days the carriage of mails by sea was a vital public service. We must not forget that telex, fax, direct dialling and e-mail did not exist. There were tight rail connections at the cross channel ports and the terms of the mail contracts included heavy penalties for delays. When the LNWR took up the Irish Mail contract, it had only the pre-war *Arvonia* and *Menavia* and the new *Curraghmore*, built for the Greenore service, which were suitable for its newly acquired route. One of my very early memories is of travelling from Holyhead by the daylight service in the summer of 1919 in the *Curraghmore*. No doubt my mother (my father was not with us on that particular journey) was sufficiently impressed by the substitution of this relatively small, albeit brand new, ship for the larger City of Dublin vessel to which she was accustomed, to mention the name to me. At the age of four and a half, I was unlikely to have been able to read it myself. Whether, at this particular time, the *Curraghmore* was on LNWR service or on charter to the CDSP Co, in its last days reduced to two vessels on account of war losses, I do not know.

The pre-war ships and the Greenore stop-gap did not last long. In 1920 and 1921 Dennys delivered what were in the opinion of many people the finest British cross channel ships of the inter-war era. The new vessels, each of which measured 381'x45', their names, gross tonnages, and delivery dates were:

Anglia	3460 grt	1920	*Scotia*	3450 grt	1921
Hibernia	3458 grt	1920	*Cambria*	3445 grt	1921

Power was provided by geared turbines driving twin screws and maximum speed was 25 knots, making the new vessels the fastest conventional craft ever to have operated commercially on the Irish Sea. Nevertheless, as far as schedules were concerned, two hours and forty-five minutes up to 1932 and about two hours and fifty-five thereafter, for the remainder of the inter-war period there was no great improvement on the timings to which the City of Dublin ships had worked. The extra ten minutes allowed for the crossing after 1932 was not due to any reduction in normal operating speed but to the fact that whereas, when the railway steamers started to operate the mail service they used the Admiralty Pier (as the CDSP Co Ships had), in 1932 their terminal was moved to the quays at the apex of the inner harbour.

These alterations provided a certain economy in the running of the 'Irish Mail' trains to and from London. When the Admiralty Pier was in use, the main line locomotives were attached to and detached from the mail trains at Holyhead Town station, a lightweight shunting engine providing the motive power between town and pier stations. Running the ships in and out of the main harbour did away with the need for the change of locomotives. Time so gained presumably balanced the extra few minutes of the sea passage. This change of berth for the mail steamers at Holyhead represented a break with the past, as well as being an economy. The name Admiralty Pier owed its origin to the fact that, in pre City of Dublin and LNWR days, mails were carried across the Irish Sea by 'Admiralty Packets'. It was not just after 1st January 1948 that state-owned transport operated at Holyhead.

To return to 1932, another change from procedures inherited from the City of Dublin Company also dated from that year. Until then, the vessel operating the day service, at about 0900 ex-Dun Laoghaire and around 1430 ex-Holyhead, ran to Holyhead and back and spent the night hours in Dun Laoghaire. The sister ship on the night turn left Dun Laoghaire at 2045, was back again at or about 0545, and then lay over in Dun Laoghaire until evening. In 1932 these rosters were altered so that the night boat from Holyhead worked the daylight service from Dun Laoghaire whilst the afternoon ship from Wales provided the evening connection from Ireland. No doubt this change was popular with the crews, who almost invariably had their homes in Holyhead or near that port. (In the 1930s it was quite common to hear Welsh spoken by members of the ships' personnel.) Minor maintenance work during lay-over periods could also be more easily carried out in the home port (though interestingly the mail steamers were registered in Dublin until 1939), where the railway company had extensive engineering facilities. More time too was available for the all important operation of coaling.

On balance the change benefited passengers, in that those travelling first class (who formed a large and important section of the clientele) and who did not wish to disembark at Holyhead at around 2330, either to face an immediate train journey or to spend a night at the station hotel, could remain in their berths until shortly before 0700 and then travel on by breakfast car train to London or elsewhere. In the opposite direction a train which left London in the late afternoon, with connections from other places, enabled one to be on board before midnight and to be in bed well before the arrival of the mail train at about 0230. In contrast to the situation at Stranraer, there were no nocturnal cargo workings to disturb one's sleep. Loading of mails was a rapid process and made little noise. A disadvantage of the new arrangements was that passengers by the morning service from Dun Laoghaire could no longer sleep on board the night before sailing. Another very early memory of mine is of my father, mother, brother and myself availing of this facility in the *Hibernia* in 1921. I cannot remember much about the actual sleeping arrangements, but I very clearly recall sitting on the boat deck on a bright summer morning, watching the arrival of the boat train from Dublin.

While on the subject of operating procedures, it may be noted that, although since the end of the Second World War the Holyhead passenger ships, both conventional and ro-ro, have normally gone astern when leaving the quaysides at either port and turned in the harbours (just outside the harbour at Dun Laoghaire in pre ro-ro days), in the inter-war years vessels always turned during the lie over periods at each port. At Holyhead, after 1932, the east side of the inner harbour was the arrival side, the site of the 1977 ro-ro berth being used for departures. At Dun Laoghaire, the west side of the Carlisle Pier (commonly known as the Mail Boat Pier) had always been the arrival side and the east side the departure one. Since there were direct rail connections at each of the four berths, the Holyhead arrangements were in accordance with normal left hand running on double track railway lines, whilst those at Dun Laoghaire reversed the process. An interesting operation at Dun Laoghaire was that, just before the departure time of the mail vessel, a small steam launch made a circuit of the harbour to ensure that the outgoing ship would have a clear passage.

Although the 1920-21 turbine steamers were considerably larger than their predecessors and namesakes, they had a fairly close superficial resemblance to them, flush-decked with a long superstructure amidships and a smaller one aft. These erections were just one deck high and had open 'promenades' on each side. Five boats, in quadrant davits, were carried on each side, four amidships and one aft. The usual tall masts and large twin funnels, so typical of Denny-built vessels, were prominent features, as were the large cowl ventilators. Despite their building dates the new ships had been designed just before the outbreak of the First World War and, indeed, the *Hibernia* and *Anglia* had been laid down by August 1914, only to have all work on them suspended for the duration of hostilities. This design date leads one to suspect that, as early as six years before the expiry of the mail contract, the LNWR had reason to expect that it would be they, and not the City of Dublin concern, who would be the chosen operators of the mail service after 1920.

As was to remain the case with the Irish Sea railway ships, until the introduction of the *Duke of York* in 1935, the standards of the third class accommodation in the new Holyhead vessels were fairly basic. First class travellers were very well provided for. (In contrast to the situation on some of the railway steamers on the English Channel routes, there was no second class.) The majority of these voyagers would be travelling 'First Boat - Third Rail', or 'Saloon and Third' as it was also called.

The main first class entrances, on the *Anglia* and her consorts, were at promenade deck level, fairly far forward in the midship structure. These entrances opened into a hall where there were the ship's bureau and the stairway to the main and lower decks. Forward of the bureau there was sleeping accommodation, consisting of 'special' and 'deck' cabins, the former situated inboard, the latter with portlights looking onto the promenade decks. Aft of the hall was the lounge, furnished with the usual heavy armchairs and sofas and provided also with a novelty in the shape of a 'coal effect' electric fire. Further aft again was the smoking room/bar. The first class dining saloon was on the main deck forward, immediately below the 'special' and 'deck' cabins. Another of my very early memories is of the vases of flowers on the saloon tables and of the silver plated candlestick type electric table lights with LNWR monograms, which remained unchanged in LMS days.

Below the dining saloon there was open-berth sleeping accommodation for 'gentlemen', where one could have the use of a berth with rug and pillow, at no extra charge above the normal fare. Aft of the dining saloon, on the starboard side of the main deck, there was an alleyway with two-berthed cabins outboard and a row of 'gentlemen's' upper and lower 'rug and pillow' berths inboard, immediately against the boiler and engine room casings. Many a time as a boy have I lain on one of these berths, an enthralled listener to the eerie moan of the boiler feed pump and, after departure, to the high pitched whine of the turbine gears. At the after end of this alleyway was the galley, whilst on the port side of the ship, aft of the saloon, was the 'ladies' cabin', presumably furnished with rug and pillow berths, though here I cannot speak from personal experience.

Although no charge was made for the use of the open berths, which were chastely provided with side curtains, there were fees of seven shillings and sixpence (37½p) for a promenade deck cabin with two fully made up berths, and five shillings (25p) for a main deck cabin with the same facilities. The fee for a 'special' cabin, with two beds in place of upper and lower berths was fifteen shillings (75p). A single berth in a two-berth cabin cost half the prices just quoted. In about 1937 the price for a single berth in a main deck cabin was increased to two shillings and ninepence, and for sole use of the cabin to five shillings and sixpence, increases of 1¼p and 2½p respectively. Many a regular traveller's head was shaken at this manifestation of galloping inflation. The official justification for the increase was that the cost of laundering bed linen had increased.

Cabins on main and promenade decks were much in demand on both day and night crossings, during the former because they provided space where people could be sick in some degree of privacy, or perhaps lie down in the hope of avoiding that ultimate horror. Seasickness was far from uncommon in the mail steamers and anticipation of it was almost universal. Fast and relatively shallow draught ships operating a tightly timed mail service, with heavy penalty provisions in case of late running, could not afford to pay too much regard to queasy stomachs. Many saloon passengers therefore sought relief, which they might or might not find, in private cabins. Others, in both first and third class, stretched themselves on open berths. Others again would spend the crossing on the seats on the open decks, many of which were of the once well known type based on a twelve person 'buoyant apparatus'. A refinement, available to those first class passengers who elected to remain on deck, was indicated by notices which announced that "Waterproof deck rugs may be hired from the steward at one shilling each". These rugs were substantial affairs, of a heavy plaid material backed by a thick waterproof fabric. I remember a similar type being used in my grandparents' pony trap.

In 1932, coincidentally with the changes in rostering, and a year after the *Princess Margaret* had demonstrated the popularity of the glassed-in observation shelter at the forward end of the boat deck, and of the forced-draught ventilation in sleeping cabins, these features were incorporated in refits given to the *Hibernia*, *Scotia* and *Cambria*. Additionally the forward ends of the promenade decks on each side of these three ships were glassed in.

The *Anglia* was not refitted, as she had been withdrawn from service in the

World Ship Society

The mail steamer *Cambria* of 1921, pictured at some time after its 1932 refit. This LMS vessel was 3445 grt and had the same overall dimensions as her three sisters, 381' x 45'.

Sean Kennedy/Green studios

The *Hibernia* of 1920 lying alongside the departure side of Carlisle Pier, Dun Laoghaire – the Mailboat Pier. Note the glassed in forward end of the promenade deck and the enclosed shelter below and forward of the bridge. These features were acquired during the vessel's major refit in 1932. With a gross tonnage of 3458 the *Hibernia* had the same overall dimensions as her three sisters in the mail service.

1920s and laid up at Barrow, where she remained until she was scrapped in 1935. A factor leading to the *Anglia*'s premature death was probably the increased reliability of the more modern vessels, as compared to that of their turn-of-the-century predecessors. I remember an occasion in the early 1930s when, with one ship in dry dock and another suddenly withdrawn for essential emergency repairs, the *Cambria* maintained the service of four single crossings, each twenty four hours, until one of her sisters was operative again. Intensive usage of this nature is normal with present day diesel-engined vessels, but it was something of a tour de force for a coal-fired steamship. The reason why the *Anglia* was not scrapped until 1935 is probably that she might have been required at some time as back-up cover for the Holyhead service, in an extreme emergency. However, the acquisition of the *Duke of York* at Heysham in 1935 made it unnecessary to retain the *Anglia*. That the *Anglia*, just fourteen years old and little used, was scrapped in 1935 and not sold for further service, is an interesting commentary on the specialised work and the unusually high and costly performance of the mail steamers.

The *Scotia* was lost with many of her crew at Dunkirk in 1940. A brass plaque on a wall of the waiting room of the 1977 ro-ro terminal at Holyhead commemorates that sad event.

Towards the end of the Second World War, the *Cambria* worked on the Belfast-Heysham service, together with the British and Irish Steam Packet Company's *Louth*. Throughout the war, the *Hibernia* continued to operate on the route for which she had been built, making one round trip per day, often for long periods without relief. For part of the time, this service was a daylight one, thus providing a return to the pre-1932 custom of the day vessel lying overnight in Dun Laoghaire. After the end of the war, the *Cambria* returned as consort to the *Hibernia* but, as a result of the fuel crisis early in 1947, the *Princess Maud*, now converted to oil firing, took over the Holyhead-Dun Laoghaire service, reduced again to one sailing per day in each direction. Later in the year, with coal once more available, the two old ships resumed service and twice daily sailings were restored, though now the 'day boat' ran in summer only. In 1949 the badly run down *Hibernia* and *Cambria* were replaced by two new and much larger (though slower) motor vessels bearing the same names. However, before going on to say something about the new *Hibernia* and *Cambria*, I would like to round off this account of the inter-war Holyhead-Dun Laoghaire ships on a personal note. I last travelled in one of these never-to-be-forgotten vessels in the summer of 1948, making the return crossing by the *Cambria*, on the night service in each direction, and so ending an association which had begun with the *Hibernia* twenty-six years earlier. At the time of these last crossings I was not to know that I was to have an almost equally long, and even closer, association with the new motor ships, to which we must now turn our attention.

By the year 1938, even though the inter-war *Cambria*, *Hibernia* and *Scotia* were only 17-18 years old, the London, Midland and Scottish Railway was formulating plans for their replacement by two large turbine-engined ships. Since these vessels were to have had a maximum service speed of 21 knots, as compared to the 25 knots of the existing ships, it would seem that by the late 1930s it was envisaged that, in the future, transport of first class mail across the Irish Sea would be by air, rather than by the faithful steamships. By 1938 Railway Air Services, an organisation owned jointly by the main line British railway companies, flew between Belfast and both Liverpool and Glasgow, whilst Aer Lingus, which had been established in 1936, was operating regularly on a route from Dublin to Bristol. The planes involved in these services were, by today's standards, both small and slow. Nevertheless, their introduction was an unmistakable sign that an era was about to end. The mail contract was due for renewal in, I think, 1940 and no doubt the LMS felt that, in view of its involvement in Railway Air Services, it had a good chance of retaining a sizeable stake in any new arrangements with the postal authorities. However, it is likely that the Irish Government (which was not in existence when the expiring contract was negotiated) would have insisted on a proportionate share of the service being provided by Aer Lingus.

However, war came; the proposed turbine vessels were never built and the 1920-21 vessels continued to carry the mails between Holyhead and Dun Laoghaire for several more years, even though, in the early years of the war, the Northern Ireland traffic was diverted to Stranraer and to some extent Heysham. Strangely, despite the partition of Ireland in 1921, most of the Northern Ireland mails had, up to then, continued to be routed via Holyhead.

Eventually, in 1949, the Holyhead-Dun Laoghaire route got its new ships: MS *Hibernia* and MS *Cambria* each of 4972 grt, and with dimensions of 397'x 54'. Motive power on twin screws was provided by a pair of Burmeister and Wain/H&W diesels, which gave a maximum service speed of 21 knots. The ships were built by Harland and Wolff at Belfast. These vessels had relatively short forecastles, and long raised midship structures comprising boat, promenade and upper decks, which were also designated A, B and C. There was a short poop house, with open alleyways, on each side. Five boats per side were carried in overhead gravity davits. All passenger accommodation was amidships and, for the first time in the history of the Irish Sea railway vessels, steerage passengers were provided with facilities approximating to the standards of the first class accommodation. This break with tradition reflected the more egalitarian structure of society which was emerging in the later 1940s, a development which, as we will see, seems not to have been fully appreciated by the Coast Lines combine.

I will not attempt to give a detailed description of the interiors of the 1949 *Hibernia* and *Cambria*, since they underwent two major alterations during the twenty-five odd years of their ownership by British Rail. Suffice it to say that there was an ample provision of lounge, bar, catering and sleeping accommodation which, particularly as regards the first two facilities, had no very great difference in standards or appearance between the two classes. At

Sean Kennedy/Green studios

The British Rail motor ship *Cambria* of 1949 coming alongside Carlisle Pier, Dun Laoghaire, after crossing from Holyhead. This product of Harland and Wolff's Belfast shipyard had a gross tonnage and main dimensions similar to those of her sister *Hibernia* – 4972 grt and 397'x 54'.

each of the two refits, additional space was allotted to third class at the expense of first, to the extent that, in their final phase, the vessels were virtually one class ships, with only a small amount of first class accommodation. This feature was particularly apparent on A and B (respectively boat and promenade) decks, where wire grill gates restricted the saloon passengers to a minute area of open space. One needs, of course, to look no further than the growth of air travel to understand why these changes were made. The maximum passenger capacity of the ships varied slightly from time to time. So far as I remember the peak figure was 2200 for "a short international voyage not exceeding ten hours in duration," to quote the wording on the combined passenger and safety certificate. A major improvement, which was carried out during the first refit, was the provision of stabilisers.

I have already mentioned that, after the fuel crisis of early 1947, the day service between Dun Laoghaire and Holyhead operated during the summer months only. This reduction resulted in what some might consider to have been an uneconomic use of the new ships during the greater part of the year, in that each vessel made just a single one way crossing every night (three hours and a quarter running time, twenty minutes longer than before September 1939), out of each twenty-four hours. However the situation was not quite so bad as it seemed at first sight, since 'sleep-on-board' facilities were available in each direction. These were popular with those first class passengers for whom time was not of the essence. As virtually all of my many crossings in the new *Hibernia* and *Cambria* were made when travelling on business as a saloon passenger, I had very little opportunity to see what proportion of third class passengers remained on board after arrival at Holyhead, or boarded the ship in the same port up to three or four hours before departure. I have already mentioned the rail services which facilitated the use of these sleeping arrangements and these services were reinstated soon after the end of the war.

As regards the actual saloon sleeping facilities, these were available in single and two-berth, as well as multi-berth, cabins and also in open dormitories. No longer, however, were berths in the latter apartments available free, as in pre-war days. As built, the ships had some very pleasant airy cabins forward on C deck but, after the second refit, these were sacrificed in the general reduction of saloon accommodation, with the result that one was generally consigned to E deck. Here, not only was the atmosphere usually somewhat warm, despite the forced draught ventilation, but the situation of the cabins was close to some unit of auxiliary machinery (I never discovered its exact function) which commenced operation shortly after one had fallen asleep on the sailing ex-Holyhead. If for no other reason than the noisy operation of this piece of machinery and, even though I was very fond of and, for many years, a regular traveller in BR's motor vessels, I was never disappointed if, on any occasion during the early part of the year (the normal period for the annual surveys), arrival of the 'Emerald Isle' through-train from London at about 2230 revealed the *Princess Maud* alongside the departure quay.

The cabin fittings in the *Hibernia* and *Cambria* were still fairly traditional in style and material, with polished hardwood bed or bunk boards, exposed electric wiring and even the time honoured hook above a velvet pad at the head of every berth, on which the 'gentleman' passenger could hang his watch. Nevertheless, despite noisy auxiliary machinery and warm air, a night crossing (first class) by the Dun Laoghaire route, making use of the 'sleep-on-board' arrangements, could be a very pleasant experience, particularly if travelling eastwards, when the auxiliary machinery was silent when the ship was berthed at Holyhead. In the absence of first class mail traffic, though parcel post and newspapers continued to be carried, the previous tight rail connections at each end had been eased considerably and so one had ample time for an evening meal after embarkation at Dun Laoghaire. The continuation of travel restrictions for some years after 1945, necessitating the examination of documents at Holyhead, was also a factor in this connection. After the meal, a stroll on the open boat deck or glassed-in 'promenade', according to weather and time of year, would be followed by a spell of reading — or maybe just a period of suspended animation, if one had been particularly busy earlier in the day — before it was time to leave the comfort of the armchair and take a look at Holyhead harbour and the vessels there, before going to bed. In the morning there was the Up 'Emerald Isle' and breakfast, whilst running through Anglesey and along the coast of north Wales, a journey whose attractions included the combination of the sea and mountain scenery of the area.

During their quarter century of service with British Rail, the *Cambria* and *Hibernia* rarely left the route for which they had been built. One of them, the *Hibernia* so far as I remember, put in a short spell on the ex-LNER connection between Harwich and the Hook of Holland and I once saw the *Cambria* in Belfast, working the Heysham service. Each of these diversions from normal operation occurred during the early 1950s. It is possible that, in the case of the *Cambria*, the vessel may have made a few trips on the Heysham service immediately after, or before, a spell at her builders' yard for her first major refit. However I have no direct evidence to support this surmise. Certainly, if the ship was visiting Harland and Wolff's at the time I saw her at Donegall Quay, Belfast, it would only have been for major work to be carried out (possibly for the installation of stabilisers, which was done at the first refit). Routine dockings, for annual survey and other purposes, were normally carried out by BR's own staff in the private dry dock at Holyhead. Not the least interesting aspect of travelling through the Welsh port in British Rail days, was that almost always there was a ship in the dry dock, often one from the English Channel or other 'foreign' area which otherwise might not have been encountered outside of the pages of reference books.

There was one diversion of the motor ships from Holyhead which lasted for an appreciable time and whose cause was as bizarre as it was unprecedented. In the early Spring of 1970 some children, engaged in the horrifying pastime of looking for birds' nests inside the great tubular bridge carrying the Chester-

Holyhead railway line over the Menai Strait and using lighted newspapers as torches, succeeded in setting fire to the lining of the bridge, which was composed of old railway sleepers. Why such highly inflammable material was ever used for lining the structure (the sleepers having originally been impregnated with creosote or other tar-based preservative) must remain a mystery but, whatever the reason, the ensuing fire was so intense that the wrought iron tubes, which had been in place since 1850, were so badly buckled that the bridge had to be rebuilt. This process took a couple of years, during which Heysham replaced Holyhead as the eastern terminus of the Dun Laoghaire route, with a resultant significant increase in crossing time. I once travelled from Heysham to Dun Laoghaire, in the summer of 1971. Other than the longer journey, there was little to differentiate the passage from the many I had made from Holyhead.

Although the purpose built ro-ro turbine steamer *Holyhead Ferry One* (an uninspired name if ever there was one – what would have been wrong with the historic *Anglia* or *Scotia*?) came onto the route in 1966, the *Cambria* and *Hibernia* continued their traditional crossings and re-crossings until 1974, when they were sold to Saudi Arabian owners for further use. The *Hibernia* was the last to go. During her final summer she was worked harder than ever before, making two round trips per day, a far cry from the leisurely existence of most of her life when, for the greater part of the year, one single passage per twenty-four hours was the norm.

Although the *Princess Maud* was the regular standby ship at Holyhead from 1947 to 1965, other vessels occasionally appeared on relief duties during those eighteen years, including the 1956 *Duke of Argyll* and the Fishguard and Rosslare *Saint Patrick* of 1948. Incidentally the *Saint Patrick* was my favourite post-war railway vessel. Additionally, both the *Duke of York* and the ex-Southern Railway *Isle of Sark* put in brief spells as summer extras during the 1950s. From 1966 until the introduction of the large purpose-built ro-ro vessel *Saint Columba* (7836 grt, 129.22m x 21.24m, built in Denmark by Aalborg Werftin in 1977), a number of car-carrying vessels operated on the Holyhead-Dun Laoghaire route but, since these were all ro-ro ships, either purpose built or conversions, they call for little further comment here, other than to list the names of some of them.

I feel, however, that three of the so called 'car ferries' which appeared in Dun Laoghaire do call for some comment. The first of these was the *Avalon*, noteworthy for being the last conventional vessel to be put into service by British Rail. This ship came onto the Eastern Region's overnight service between Harwich and the Hook of Holland in 1963. As well as being the largest ever railway passenger steamer, she is remembered as having been designed for cruising, as well as for regular cross-channel service. She did indeed make a number of short cruises to eastern North Sea and Baltic ports but, like the 1956 'Dukes', she had been built at least a decade too late and her career in the services for which she had been designed was short. In 1969, she was converted into a ro-ro ship, a process which reduced her gross tonnage from 6584 to 5152.

In about 1971, she was transferred to the Fishguard-Rosslare service but, a few years later, took up residence at Holyhead, where she remained until her sale to a Cypriot company in 1980. Not long afterwards, she was sold again, this time to Indian ship-breakers. It is conceivable that, had she been diesel rather than steam powered, she might have lasted somewhat longer. I made a couple of passages in the *Avalon* during her Holyhead-Dun Laoghaire days. On the first occasion I was looking forward to the trip as, in view of the origins of the vessel, I expected something rather above the average of the day as regards comfort and amenities. In the event, I was disappointed. So thorough had been the removal of the original accommodation and the subsequent refitting, that this erstwhile BR flagship resembled nothing so much as a stretched Holyhead or Dover Ferry — utilitarian vessels to say the least. However, I have a slightly bizarre memory of the *Avalon*. One winter evening, when she was working the time honoured 2045 departure ex-Dun Laoghaire, passengers had to board via the link span at the stern, on account of extreme tidal conditions preventing normal operation of the side gangway. As we made our way up the dirty and narrow companionway from the car deck to the passenger accommodation, an obviously bewildered man turned to me and said "Are we on the ship yet?"

The second ro-ro ship which I wish to mention is the *Mona's Queen*, this time not on account of anything special about her history or origins, but merely on account of the fact that she appeared on a Sealink (as the erstwhile BR Marine services had become) route at all — a fact which, even three or four years before its occurrence, would have been unimaginable. The *Mona's Queen*, one of the last two vessels built for the independent Isle of Man Steam Packet Company (the other was her somewhat younger sister *Lady of Mann*), was a diesel-engined vessel of 2998 tonnes, whose main dimensions were 104.45m x16.74m. She was a purpose built ro-ro ship but, in order that she could operate on any of her company's routes, some of which were 'summer only' to and from ports without link spans, she was designed as a side loader. In the stern of the vessel there was a three-level skeletal erection, onto one of whose levels cars could be driven directly from the quayside, the level used depending on the state of the tide. A spiral arrangement, resembling a ramp in a multi storey car park, connected the various levels and the car deck amidships. Apart from the stern erection, the *Mona's Queen* resembled a conventional cross channel passenger ship in external appearance.

For a very short period in 1987, Sealink, which by that time had acquired a controlling interest in the IOMSP Co, chartered the *Mona's Queen* as a replacement for the *Saint Columba* when the latter vessel had unexpectedly to be withdrawn for essential repairs. It so happened that my wife and I were on our way back to Dublin from a short holiday in England. (It was the time that we went to Parkgate and observed the beached *Duke of Lancaster* in the far distance.) We were travelling as 'foot passengers' and were booked on the late afternoon British and Irish sailing from Holyhead, since we had been informed that Sealink had no sailing on that day, due to the *Saint Columba*'s mishap. However,

(Continued on page 55)

Barry Carse

Saint Andrew, 1932, alongside Carlisle Pier, Dun Laoghaire. Note the initials 'FR' on the funnel, which dates the picture to 1966 or 1967. One wonders why this ship was in Dun Laoghaire. Possibly she had been operating an excursion for Welsh rugby fans on the occasion of an international match in Dublin.

Brian Boyle

The Fishguard and Rosslare Railways and Harbours Company's turbine steamer *Saint David*, 3352 grt and built by Cammell Laird in 1947, arriving at Rosslare. The date is 1966 or later, as evidenced by the initials 'FR' on the funnel. By this time *Saint David* had been converted to a side loading car carrier.

Barry Carse

Hibernia, in her last days, alongside the traditional departure side of Carlisle Pier, Dun Laoghaire in December 1975. Built in 1949, she is seen here in BR 'Sealink' livery and makes interesting comparison with *Cambria*, seen on the front cover twelve years earlier.

Barry Carse

Lord Warden, 3332 grt, delivered by Dennys in 1952, was the first of British Rail's purpose built ro-ro ships. For many years she was based at Dover but, towards the end of her life, operated on relief and 'extra' services where required. This picture shows *Lord Warden* in Dun Laoghaire harbour, when the vessel was on the short-lived summer service from Fishguard, in 1978. The two black balls at the top of the main mast indicate that the vessel is proceeding astern into her berth.

H S Corran

Mona's Queen, built in 1971. This was the third of the four ro-ro ships built for the IOMSP Co during its separate existance.

when we arrived at Holyhead by train from Chester, we found that *Mona's Queen* was all set to take the scheduled Sealink sailing to Dun Laoghaire. There was no love lost between B and I and Sealink in those days and, in marked contrast to the situation in former times, tickets were not interchangeable. Nevertheless we succeeded in arguing our way on to the *Mona's Queen*, on the not unreasonable grounds that we had B and I tickets only because British Rail in Chester had told us that there was no Sealink service. So we experienced, not merely the only passage from Holyhead to Dun Laoghaire that either of us had ever made in an Isle of Man vessel, but also the fastest post-war journey that I experienced between the two ports. As for the *Mona's Queen*, she was reasonably fast, moderately comfortable and exhibited the usual dirty and uncared for appearance that has become all too common since the introduction of intensive usage and multi-crewing.

When *Mona's Queen* arrived at Dun Laoghaire, we found a stranger lying alongside the ro-ro pier. This was the *Earl William*, an ex Viking vessel, one of the original Thoresen ships from the Dover-Calais service, subsequently acquired and renamed by Sealink, primarily to operate between Weymouth and Jersey and Guernsey (shades of the two *Saint Patricks*), but which was about to inaugurate a new Sealink service between Dun Laoghaire and Liverpool. This venture was embarked on by Sealink after the British and Irish had abandoned Liverpool as their English terminus of the Dublin service, in favour of Holyhead, an operation to which we will make a further brief reference later in our story. *Earl William*, 3670 grt, 313' x 57' 6", dating from 1964, did not stay long on the Irish Sea. The new service, which operated during the summer only, was withdrawn at the end of the 1988 season. However, during that year, we travelled via Dun Laoghaire-Liverpool en route to Inverness and, in an ex-Norwegian ship at that, a most unexpected experience and one which, a few years earlier, I would have rated as just as unlikely as arriving from Holyhead in an IOMSP Co vessel. My main memory of this two way trip concerns the return passage when, on going on deck early in the morning, I saw a ship some distance astern but obviously gaining on us despite our alleged 18 knots. The vessel was soon identified as the B and I *Tipperary*, 3043 tonnes, 150.02m x 20.73m, a ro-ro freighter on her regular Liverpool-Dublin shuttle service. The *Tipperary* overtook us close by on our port side. I watched her until she was well away towards the western horizon and then went below for some breakfast, reflecting that maybe this was the last laugh in the old CDSP Co/LNWR rivalry and that the laugh was on the CDSP Co, in that a cargo vessel belonging to its lineal descendant, the B and I, was showing her heels to one of the passenger ships of the LNWR's successor in title. That was my last passage from Liverpool to an Irish port and is likely to remain so. On that account and, on account of the unusual routing and the 'foreign' ship, the crossing will not be forgotten.

Other ro-ro ships, as well as *Holyhead Ferry One* and *Avalon* which appeared at Dun Laoghaire from time to time, included *Dover*, a near twin of *Holyhead Ferry*; *Lord Warden*, the first purpose built ro-ro vessel for BR's English Channel services, built in 1952 and which had a gross tonnage of 3332 and measured 361' x 59'1"; *Maid of Kent*, built in 1969 for the Dover-Boulogne service, and considered to be very much state of the art at the time of her introduction. However, by the time my wife and I made a return crossing to Holyhead in her in the autumn of 1980 she was badly run down, dirty and generally unattractive; *Duke of Rothesay* and *Saint David*, each of which was a conversion from a conventional vessel. Also, for very brief periods towards the end of the 1980s, two more Southerners appeared:- *Saint Eloi*, built as a train ferry, and *Earl Granville*. These ships, of 4469 and 4478 grt respectively, dated from 1974 and 1973. On the evidence of Barry Carse's striking picture (page 71), *Ailsa Princess* also operated on the Holyhead-Dun Laoghaire route at the same time, though I do not remember having seen her at Dun Laoghaire. None of these vessels put in any long service, and indeed *Lord Warden* appeared only in 1971 on a short lived Fishguard-Dun Laoghaire summer operation.

FISHGUARD-ROSSLARE

It is now time for us to consider that jointly owned and long titled subsidiary of the Great Western and Great Southern and Western Railways, the 'Fishguard and Rosslare Railways and Harbours Company'. Although this concern was the legal owner of the turbine steamships which ran between Fishguard in Pembrokeshire and Rosslare in Co Wexford, the vessels were operated as part of the Great Western's fleet. Nevertheless, on account of the joint parentage of the F&RR&H Co, the Fishguard and Rosslare service provided the only example of the participation of an Irish railway company in an Irish Sea passenger service. In contrast to LNWR/LMS practice the F&R vessels were manned by mixed British/Irish crews.

The story of the rivalries, negotiations and, eventually, legislation, which culminated in the setting up of the Rosslare route in 1906, is a fascinating piece of railway history, but has no place in a narrative dealing primarily with ships. In the 1920s, the service across the fifty-four nautical miles between the Welsh and Irish ports was maintained by three direct-drive triple-screw turbine ships, *Saint Patrick* and *Saint David*, each built in 1906, with main dimensions of 350'x 41' and a gross tonnage of 2460, and *Saint Andrew*, which dated from 1908, measured 351'x 41' and had a gross tonnage of 2495. These vessels, which had a very distinctive appearance. with two large funnels and high forecastles and had been built at John Brown's Clydebank yard, carried saloon and third class passengers, parcels and perishable cargo, including much agricultural produce from Ireland. The standard time for the passage was just under three hours and, as there was direct rail communication at the quaysides to and from London and other British cities, on the one hand, and Cork and elsewhere in Ireland, on the other, the service provided significant competition to the Holyhead route for traffic from and to the southern parts of Ireland, south Wales and the south and west of England. Until August 1914 there were both day and night crossings in each direction but, during inter-war days, the regular service was once each way

World Ship Society

Saint Patrick, 1922 grt, 281'x 41', built in 1930, was the second vessel of the name to work on the Fishguard-Rosslare route. She was intended to act as a standby and relief ship on both the Fishguard-Rosslare and the Weymouth-Channel Islands services. She is pictured here at Weymouth.

every week-night, with extra sailings at peak periods.

There had been a fourth F&R ship, the *Saint George*, delivered by Browns in 1908, which was generally similar to the other three but she was soon sold to Canadian interests, who disposed of her to the Great Eastern Railway in 1913. Presumably it was found that, as was the case at Holyhead a couple of decades later, three turbine vessels were adequate to maintain the double daily service. *Saint Patrick* was disposed of in 1929, after a fire, but was replaced in the following year by a namesake, a single-funnelled geared-turbine vessel which was designed to operate on either the Rosslare or the Channel Island routes. This ship, Clyde-built like her predecessor but by Alexander Stephen and Company, was smaller than the 1906 vessel, 1922 grt with main measurements of 281'x 41'.

In 1932 a new *Saint Andrew* and a new *Saint David* came from Cammell Laird's Birkenhead yard. Their elderly forerunners, which for a while had been running under the names of *Fishguard* (*Saint Andrew*) and *Rosslare* (*Saint David*), were then scrapped. It is interesting to note that, whilst the LNWR, and subsequently the LMS, were consistent clients of Dennys (the pioneers of the fast turbine-engined cross channel vessel), the Great Western/F&R Co were apparently believers in the merits of shopping around.

The new geared-turbine ships were very different in appearance from the 1906/08 vessels. Shorter and broader, 327'x 47', they had single funnels, cruiser

World Ship Society

The *Saint Andrew* of 1932, 2702 grt, 327'x 47', the sole survivor of the three Fishguard-Rosslare ships of the later inter-war years. Note the tripod mast which she acquired during her post-war refit. This refit resulted in an increase of gross tonnage to 3035.

sterns, had the forward ends of their promenade decks glassed in and carried their boats partly in gravity and partly in quadrant davits. The gross tonnage of each vessel was 2702. I never knew these steamers in the inter-war years (though I remember seeing one of their predecessors at Rosslare in 1930), but I came to know the *Saint Andrew* well over the twenty years from 1947. This was after the ship's extensive post-war refit, which increased the gross tonnage to 3035 and replaced the conventional foremast, on the wall deck, by a tripod aft of the bridge.

Of the three Rosslare-Fishguard ships which were in service in the summer of 1939, only the *Saint Andrew* survived the war. The *Saint Patrick*, after surviving several earlier attacks, was sunk by a German bomber whilst on passage Rosslare-Fishguard in June 1941. The *Saint David* was lost in 1944 when serving as a hospital ship in the Mediterranean. In 1940 she had taken part in the Dunkirk evacuation. The *Saint Andrew* also served as a hospital ship and, during the later war years, spent much time in the Mediterranean. Earlier, she had been the vessel involved in an exchange of seriously wounded British and German prisoners of war in 1941. The *Saint Andrew* was not released from Government service until the end of 1945, after which she spent a considerable amount of time awaiting and undergoing a major refit, before reopening the Fishguard-Rosslare service (closed since the Christmas period of 1943/44) in the early summer of 1947. This sole survivor of the three pre-war 'Saints', worked for a further twenty years on her regular route, before being withdrawn for scrapping in 1967. During the 1950s she made a couple of sailings between Fishguard and Belfast on occasions of Irish/Welsh Rugby Internationals in the latter city.

A new *Saint David* and a new *Saint Patrick* were delivered by Cammell Laird in 1947 and 1948 respectively but, by 1967, with the development of ro-ro services, the *Saint Andrew* was succeeded, not by a new conventional vessel but, as we have seen, by the *Duke of Rothesay*, built in 1956 for the Heysham-Belfast route but now converted into a side-loading car carrier.

I have several memories of crossings in the *Saint Andrew,* one of which, in 1966, vied with my 1938 trip in the *Princess Margaret* as being the liveliest of all the very many I made in railway steamers. I also recall how pleasant it was, late on a summer evening, having left London by an earlier train than the regular boat connection and, after an attractively scenic journey through south west Wales, to arrive on board a spotlessly clean ship and have a late supper in the airy dining room with its wide windows looking directly on to the promenade deck. Then, after a final stroll around the boat deck, observing the departure of the *Great Western* to Waterford, I would retire for a good night's sleep in one of the large single cabins below the bridge. The charge for this accommodation (far surpassing what was on offer on 'E' deck on the *Cambria* or *Hibernia*), was relatively modest and one's employers never queried the expense account.

So much, for the moment, for the *Saint Andrew*. Now let us take a look at the 1947 and 1948 additions to the Fishguard fleet. The post-war *Saint Patrick* and *Saint David* are better described as 'cousin' rather than sister ships. They had the same overall dimensions, 321′x 54′, each sported a single funnel and each was powered by geared-turbines driving twin-screws. However the *Saint David* was officially credited with a slightly higher maximum service speed, 20¾ knots, than the *Saint Patrick*, whose passengers had to be content with the even twenty. On the other hand, as regards gross tonnage, the *Saint Patrick* measured 3492, as against *Saint David*'s 3352. Each ship had a two-deck-high midship structure containing both the saloon and the steerage accommodation, above which three boats per side were carried in quadrant davits. However, whilst in the *Saint Patrick* the upper of these two decks had an open 'promenade' either side at the after end, and wide-windowed side lounges forward, the *Saint David*'s upper deck had a short after-promenade, but lacked the generous provision of windows found on the *Saint Patrick*.

From the resumption of the Fishguard-Rosslare service, until the early 1960s, the schedule for three quarters of the year provided for sailings on just three nights per week in each direction, with a reversion to six nights (plus extras as required) during the summer. One result of this reduction of schedules, compared to those of pre-war days, was that there was no need for a third ship to be stationed at Fishguard and so, in 1959, the *Saint Patrick* was transferred permanently to the English Channel where she worked first on the Channel

World Ship Society

Saint Patrick, 3482 grt, 321′x 50′.4″, was delivered by Cammell Laird in 1948 to the Fishguard and Rosslare Railways and Harbours Company. Unfortunately, this most attractive vessel did not remain for long on the route for which she had been designed. British Rail (as half owners of the F and R Co) transferred her permanently to the English Channel in 1959.

World Ship Society

The *Saint David*, 3352 grt, 321' x 50.4, was built by Cammell Laird for the Fishguard and Rosslare service in 1947. Towards the end of her life she was converted to a ro-ro ship, but with restricted height side loading only.

Islands and, subsequently, on the Southampton-Saint Malo and Folkestone-Boulogne routes. She was of course no stranger to Weymouth, Guernsey or Jersey as, like her namesake of 1929, she had regularly appeared in those ports since her introduction.

I have already mentioned that the *Saint Patrick* appeared as a relief vessel on the Dun Laoghaire-Holyhead route. My reaction, on hearing that she had been for all time banished to the English Channel, was that it was a pity that she had not been installed at Holyhead, and the *Princess Maud* sent south. However, my regrets notwithstanding, to the English Channel she went and remained there until 1971 when she was sold to Greek owners, who renamed her *Thermopylae*, and subsequently passed her on to another Greek firm under whose ownership (as *Agapitos One*) she lasted until the mid 1970s. So ended one of the most attractive of the post Second World War Irish Sea railway steamers which, owing to circumstances, never had a chance to prove her real worth for the clientele for whom she had been designed.

Whatever about the wanderings of the *Saint Patrick*, the *Saint David* spent virtually all of her life on the Fishguard-Rosslare service. In 1964 she was deprived of some of her sleeping accommodation in order to provide additional space for the carriage of motor cars. Since, however, these were still loaded and unloaded by crane, the only way in which the increasing summer holiday car traffic could be accommodated, without the use of a third vessel, was by conversion of the *Saint David* to ro-ro operation. This conversion was made in the following year (1965) by providing side loading facilities towards the stern of the vessel. By this time, the *Saint Andrew* was thirty years old and not considered to be worth the cost of a similar conversion and, as we have seen, she lasted only a couple more years. As regards the increase in traffic, this had started to grow appreciably at the beginning of the 1960s and, starting in 1962, the summer services were progressively augmented, with some sailings being advertised as catering for motorists only, with no rail connections at either port. Coincidentally with the *Saint David*'s being provided with drive on and off facilities, British Rail inaugurated a new 'Motorists' service between London and Fishguard, called 'The London Irish Car Carrier'. This service, which became very popular, was similar to others provided for holiday makers by BR between London and Scotland, and Scotland and the north of England to and from Channel ports.

Despite the conversion of the *Saint David*, this vessel and the *Saint Andrew* were insufficient to cope with all the traffic offering in 1966 and so the MS *Slieve Donard*, 1598 grt, 310'3 x 47'3", built in 1960 primarily for the Holyhead-Dublin (North Wall) cargo and livestock service but with capacity for 100 cars and having stern loading facilities, came to Fishguard to provide extra car accommodation during the height of the summer season. The *Slieve Donard* was a much travelled and versatile vessel. I understand that in 1961 she had frequently been in Rosslare as a container carrier and I remember seeing her once in the mid 1960s acting as an extra car carrier at Larne.

Mention of the 1960s and the extra summer car traffic reminds me that one of my most enduring memories of travelling between Rosslare and Fishguard dates from that period. In late September 1966 I journeyed from Belfast to London via that route, a procedure that few people other than ship enthusiasts would have contemplated, but one which I always appreciated on the few occasions when I had the necessary time to undertake it. When I arrived at Rosslare, by the evening train from Dublin, it was blowing very strongly from the north west. Both of the regular ships were alongside the pier, the *Saint David* working the regular 2245 service, and aft of her the *Saint Andrew*, due to leave a couple of hours later as an 'extra'. Each ship was rising and falling in the heavy swell rolling in across the outer section of Wexford Harbour, the sort of movement one often experienced to a minor degree at Fishguard but which never before, nor since, did I encounter at Rosslare. Soon after I had boarded the *Saint Andrew* word went round that, owing to the motion, loading of the *Saint David* had been suspended and that, until cars booked on that vessel had been dealt with, nothing could be done about craning the remaining vehicles on to the *Saint Andrew*. So I hired myself one of my favourite single cabins on the boat deck and went to sleep. I do not remember just what time it was when we got away, though I woke up briefly at that point, but it was probably about 0830, as it was about midday when we got to Fishguard. (The post Second World War schedules were appreciably slower than those in force before 1914.) During the intervening period the ship had wallowed her way across Saint George's Channel with that distinctive motion peculiar to vessels running before a heavy sea — down goes the bow, up comes the rudder towards the surface and over swings the stern before, as the sea passes, dipping again only to rise and swing again in the opposite direction. All the time the vessel rolls in unison with the stern movements. In this case, however, the really impressive roll was when the *Saint Andrew* turned to starboard just after entering Fishguard harbour, the like of which, on a short sea passage, I have experienced only when crossing the Roost of Sumburgh between the southern extremity of the Shetland mainland and Fair Isle, or on the Pentland Firth. No doubt, had this crossing from Rosslare been made in a winter storm, rather than in an autumn strong gale, we would have had a much more uncomfortable crossing and a livelier time still, had the journey been made in the opposite direction. Nevertheless, that trip certainly ensured that the *Saint Andrew* is one of the ships which I most clearly remember over thirty years after I last set foot in her.

A final word about the *Saint David*. I have said that this vessel spent virtually all her life on the Fishguard-Rosslare route. I used the word 'virtually' because in 1971 she appeared at Dun Laoghaire, though I saw her there only once. In view of her small car capacity (70 vehicles only) she would not have been suitable for any regular service on the Holyhead route, so I presumed that she had been brought in as a stop-gap during an emergency. This vessel was disposed of soon afterwards, having been succeeded on her regular route by the *Avalon*.

This narrative is primarily concerned with ships, and the routes on which they operated. Little is said about port facilities and connecting rail services. It seems appropriate, however, to mention the arrangements for dealing with passengers' motor cars at Rosslare since, before 1965, they were unlike any provision for loading cars at any other Irish or British cross channel port.

All the railway owned passenger services which operated on the Irish Sea after 1919, with the exception of the Dun Laoghaire-Holyhead mail route, carried motor vehicles, which were lifted on and off the vessels by shore based cranes or ships' gear. (The sole exception to this time consuming procedure was at Larne and Stranraer during the summer of 1939, and again during post-war summers, when the two *Princess Victorias* and the *Hampton Ferry* provided a ro-ro service.) On all other services, shipment of a car necessitated its being delivered at the quayside at an appreciable time, usually measured in hours, before sailing, sometimes indeed before passengers were allowed on board. Travellers from Dun Laoghaire to Holyhead had to have their vehicles conveyed by cargo ship from Dublin (North Wall) to the Welsh port, leaving them (the passengers) the choice between making their own way to Dun Laoghaire after delivering their cars at the quayside in Dublin or, in the inter-war years, of making the crossing in the cargo ship, in which there was only steerage accommodation. However, since only one of the new freight/livestock vessels delivered to the LMS from 1930 onwards catered for passengers, the chances were that, by 1937, the option of accompanying up to 700 head of cattle on the 4-4½ hour passage might not be available. A comparable state of affairs, minus bovine fellow travellers, prevailed ex-Holyhead.

Drivers and their vehicles did travel in the same ship between Rosslare and Fishguard but, since before 1965 there was no proper road along the railway viaduct which connected the mainland with the isolated breakwater/pier at Rosslare, all cars and passengers had to be brought across the gap by train. The procedure was for a rake of flat wagons to be stationed in a bay platform with hinged metal flaps providing a means of driving from one wagon to another. Cars were driven in succession onto the rearmost wagon and then forward until the entire train was loaded, after which it proceeded across the viaduct and was unloaded at a similar installation at the other end. Accommodation for car drivers and passengers was provided in an old six-wheeled coach immediately behind the locomotive, which carried out its duties in shuttle fashion, pulling from and propelling (pushing) towards the pier.

Direct access from the mainland to the breakwater/pier, together with side loading facilities for cars, was provided at Rosslare in time for the 1965 summer tourist season. The latter improvements were also provided at Fishguard. A few years later each port was equipped with conventional stern loading linkspans permitting the employment of purpose built ro-ro vessels. In recent years major improvements have been made at Rosslare, which now has regular services to Fishguard (Stena), Pembroke Dock (Irish Ferries, as successors to B and I), Le Havre (Irish Ferries and P and O) and Cherbourg (Irish Ferries).

FISHGUARD-WATERFORD

The Great Western Railway Company operated in its own right a passenger/cargo/livestock service between Fishguard and Waterford. This service was the successor to one which the company had previously maintained between New Milford and Waterford, which ceased to run when the Fishguard-Rosslare route was opened. A clause in the Act of Parliament, which established the F&RRH Co, stipulated the setting up and continuance of the Fishguard-Waterford service, a provision which led to litigation when Sealink (as successors to the GWR) abandoned the Waterford route in the 1970s.

During the earlier inter-war years the connection between Fishguard and Waterford was maintained at a frequency of three nights per week in each direction by the *Great Southern* and the *Great Western*, twin-screw reciprocating-engined steamships which had been built in 1902 and which had main dimensions of 276'x 36' and a gross tonnage of 1225 in each case. There had been a third vessel, the *Waterford*, dating from 1912, but she was sold in 1924. In 1932 the *Great Western* was chartered by a group of persons interested in the Shetland sheep trade, in an attempt to provide competition to the North of Scotland and Orkney and Shetland Steam Navigation Company, whose vessels had a

World Ship Society

The passenger/cargo/livestock steamship *Great Southern*, built in 1902 for the Great Western Railway Co's New Milford to Waterford service. From 1906 the Welsh terminal of the route was changed to Fishguard. This ship (and her sister *Great Western*) was of 1225 grt and measured 276' x 36'.

monopoly of the passenger, freight and livestock traffic between the Shetland Islands, Aberdeen and Leith. The venture was not a success and the *Great Western* rejoined her sister for a further two years on the Irish Sea.

In 1934 the two elderly sisters were replaced by a new *Great Western*, which was also a twin-screw reciprocating-engined steamship but was appreciably larger than her predecessors, at 1659 grt, and main dimensions 282'9"x 40'4". This vessel carried first and third class passengers and general cargo, but earned her keep largely as a cattle ship. She was of conventional design with a long midship superstructure, carried out to the full width of the hull, and with a small additional erection, which housed the saloon entrance, immediately below the bridge. The third class accommodation, which was situated aft, was entered via a poop house, on either side of which were short open side-decks. The *Great Western* survived the war — during which, in 1944, she ran briefly in Government service — and then remained on the Waterford route until 1967, though during her last few years she did not carry passengers. She was replaced by a British Rail container vessel for the remaining years during which the service operated. It is likely that the busiest year of the *Great Western*'s life, as far as passenger carrying was concerned, was the twelve months between the start of the summer season of 1946 and that of the following year. Passenger carrying to and from Waterford was reinstated in the former year, whilst, as we have seen, it was 1947 before pre-war facilities were restored to Rosslare. During the intervening

World Ship Society

The Great Western Railway Company's *Great Western*, 1659 grt, 282.9 x 40'4", built in 1934. This ship single handedly maintained the company's Fishguard-Waterford service, with gaps during the war years, until 1967. Note the high bridge, an unusual feature for a vessel of her type.

period the *Great Western* frequently sailed with her full complement of travellers. I know of only two other diversions of this little ship from the Waterford route. The first was between April 1941 (when the *Saint Patrick* was lost) and December 1943, during which time she made some sailings to and from Rosslare, and again for a period during 1965 and 1966, when she again served Rosslare from Fishguard, but this time carrying loaded meat containers from Ireland, en route to London, and empties on the return passage.

Finally as regards the *Great Western* of 1934 there is one episode of her career that deserves to be mentioned. During a crossing from Fishguard at some time in the 1950s (I am afraid that I have forgotten the exact date), the ship was many hours overdue into Waterford, nor had anything been heard from her. It was beginning to be feared that she had been overcome by the exceptionally bad weather when, eventually, she was seen rounding 'The Hook' and making her way up the Suir Estuary past Dunmore East and Ballyhack. So great had been the force of the storm that not only had the ship's boats been carried away but the radio transmission gear had been put out of action. My recollection is that the newspaper reports of this ordeal stated that there were only five passengers on board. No doubt, during the hectic crossing, these unfortunates had arrived at the classic state of fearing, not that they were going to die, but that they might not achieve that blessed relief to their sufferings.

In contrast to the situation at most other ports served by directly owned passenger railway steamers, there was no rail connection to Adelphi Wharf, Waterford, the quay used by the Fishguard steamer. The port is situated on each side of the River Suir at some considerable distance from the open sea. The erstwhile Waterford North (now Plunkett) station is on the north bank of the river, whereas the Fishguard berth was on the south side, some way downstream from the road bridge which led from the railway station to the south quays. It was a great pity that the *Great Western* and her forebears could not have berthed on the north bank of the river close to the station since, at the time with which we are dealing, no fewer than five lines of railway, all with regular passenger services, converged on Waterford North.

DUBLIN-SILLOTH

In the introduction to this narrative I mentioned the service between Dublin and Silloth which was operated by William Sloan and Company and I stated that the North British Railway Company and, subsequently, the London and North Eastern had an interest in it. Operation of this route dated back to the nineteenth century and, over the years, various interests and ownerships were involved. For almost all of the 1920s Sloans ran the service, using the single screw steamship *Yarrow*, built in 1893 with a gross tonnage of 903 and main dimensions of 286'x 32'. The *Yarrow* had the conventional nineteenth century layout of passenger accommodation, with saloon passengers aft and third class forward. There were midship and after superstructures with open alleyways on either side, whilst saloon passengers anxious to benefit from sea breezes were afforded some space on the top of the after superstructure. Since however, the ship was more of a cattle carrier than a passenger vessel, having a considerable amount of livestock space in the twin decks, I doubt very much if even the

Alan Brown's collection

William Sloan and Company's *Yarrow*, built in 1893, 903 grt, 286' x 32', which was renamed *Assaroe* after the formation of the Dublin and Silloth Steamship Company in 1929. The picture shows the vessel entering Silloth docks at some time before her change of ownership. Note the open bridge, in later years the vessel had a wheelhouse.

strongest wafts of ozone would have been able to dispel the all pervading stockyard aroma. This doubt is based on my experience of travel in other ships of the same general type as the *Yarrow*, though regrettably never in that vessel herself.

In 1929 William Sloan and Company withdrew from the Dublin-Silloth route but a new concern, the Dublin and Silloth Steamship Company, was established, largely through the efforts of the Irish Livestock Exporters Association, whose members were perturbed by the threat of closure of the most direct route from Ireland to the important cattle markets in Carlisle and the south of Scotland. The D&SS Co took over the *Yarrow*, which was renamed *Assaroe* and had her funnel colours changed from black with two white bands, to buff with a black top, beneath which was a narrow green band. Management of the *Assaroe* was entrusted to the Dublin firm of Palgrave, Murphy and Co, which had links with the Head Line (G Heyn and Co) of Belfast. The only vessel other than the *Assaroe* which I ever saw on the Silloth service was a Head Line ship, from memory the *Wicklow Head*, in about 1932.

The name *Yarrow* was in accordance with Sloans' practice of naming their vessels after Scottish rivers, (others were *Brora*, *Beauly* and *Findhorn*). *Assaroe*, though not the name of an Irish river, related directly to one, being the name of the falls on the River Erne at Ballyshannon, Co Donegal.

After the change of owners, the Dublin and Silloth service continued to operate as before, with departures from Dublin on Mondays and Thursdays and from Silloth on Wednesdays and Saturdays, calling at Douglas, Isle of Man, in each direction and thus providing the only all the year round regular service from Dublin to the Island. The service was basically a night one, although departure and arrival times varied in accordance with tidal conditions at Silloth.

The outbreak of the Second World War had no immediate effect on the *Assaroe*'s bi-weekly crossings of the Irish Sea, though she came under attack from a German plane at least once, happily without suffering any casualties. In 1942 the old ship was put to run between Dublin and Lisbon and, after the war, she continued to operate sporadically on Palgrave Murphy's Irish/Continental services until 1947. In that year, having suffered severe weather in the Bay of Biscay, she was withdrawn and broken up at the respectable age of fifty-four. I understand that her troubles in the Bay culminated in her being 'pooped', with resultant flooding of her saloon accommodation, which by then was in use solely by ship's personnel. The regular Dublin-Silloth service was never reinstated after the war, although occasional shipments of cattle were made from Dublin until the 1970s.

I have not been able to determine the exact nature of the interest of the LNER in the D&SS Co. In the purely financial sense it may well have been small. However, as the owner of Silloth docks, the railway company was a vital factor in D&SS operations. The company was sufficiently involved in the shipping service to publish, and exhibit on its stations each month, current timetables showing departure and arrival times of the *Assaroe*, together with rail connections with the main Scottish and northern English towns. These timetables were exhibited at some Irish railway stations as well as British ones.

SUMMARY OF RAILWAY COMPANIES' SERVICES

It is now time to summarise the position as regards the railways' Irish Sea passenger services and the ships which operated them at the beginning of August 1939, and also at the end of 1961, the year before the introduction of the *Caledonian Princess* .

SHIPS NORMALLY IN USE ON EACH ROUTE, 1939

Stranraer-Larne (LMS)
Princess Maud   1934
Princess Victoria   1939

Heysham-Belfast (LMS)
Duke of Argyll   1928
Duke of Lancaster   1928
Duke of Rothesay   1928
Duke of York   1935
Princess Margaret 1931
(also relieved at Stranraer)

Holyhead-Dublin (3rd class only) **(LMS)**
Slieve Donard   1921
Slieve More   1932

Holyhead-Dun Laoghaire (LMS)
Hibernia   1920
Cambria   1921
Scotia   1921

Fishguard-Rosslare (F&RR&H Co)
Saint Andrew   1932
Saint David   1932
Saint Patrick   1930
(also ran on GWR Channel Islands route)

Fishguard-Waterford (GWR)
Great Western   1934

Dublin-Douglas-Silloth (D&SS Co)
Assaroe   1892

NOTE ON HULL AND FUNNEL COLOURS AND PORTS OF REGISTRY

All of the above vessels had black hulls. All except *Assaroe* had white upper-works. *Assaroe's* upper-works were a light sand colour. LMS ships had buff funnels with black tops. Vessels of the F and R Co and of the GWR had red, black topped funnels. *Assaroe's* funnel was buff with a black top, beneath which was a narrow green band. Stranraer based ships were registered at that port. Heysham vessels were registered at Lancaster, though *Princess Margaret* kept her Stranraer registration. Holyhead ships were registered in Dublin until the outbreak of war and, subsequently, in London. London was also the port of registry of the Fishguard 'Saints' and of the *Great Western*. As *Yarrow*, the *Assaroe* was registered in Glasgow but, after her change of name and ownership, her home port became Dublin. Most Irish registered ships flew the British Red Ensign until the outbreak of war, though none of course did so during the conflict, or subsequently.

SHIPS NORMALLY IN USE ON EACH ROUTE, DECEMBER 1961

Stranraer-Larne (British Rail)
Princess Margaret 1931
Extra summer service operated by
Hampton Ferry (1934)

Heysham-Belfast (British Rail)
Duke of Argyll 1956
Duke of Lancaster 1956
Duke of Rothesay 1956

Fishguard-Waterford (British Rail)
Great Western 1934

Fishguard-Rosslare (F&RR&H Co)
Saint Andrew 1932
Saint David 1947

Holyhead-Dun Laoghaire (British Rail)
Cambria 1949
Hibernia 1949
Princess Maud 1934
(also relieved at Stranraer)

NOTE ON HULL AND FUNNEL COLOURS

The above noted ships were the regular vessels but, as a result of nationalisation of the railways, other ships occasionally appeared at Stranraer and Holyhead, whilst the *Princess Maud*, at one time or another, served on all five routes listed above. Hull and funnel colours in 1961 were the same as they had been in 1939, with the exception of the *Great Western* which, on the inception of nationalisation in 1948, had had its red funnel with black top changed to buff with black top.

It was not until 1964 that Sealink (as British Rail's marine division became known) adopted the livery of blue hulls, white upper-works and red funnels, with the railway logo in white painted on the latter. It was in 1964 too, that *Saint Andrew* and *Saint David*, the last ships to be registered under the ownership of the F&RR&H Co, had the letters F R, in white, painted on their funnels — an addition which in no way improved the appearance of the vessels.

Barry Carse

The 1971 Italian-built *Ailsa Princess*, originally a Larne-Stranraer vessel, leaving Dun Laoghaire for Holyhead on I June 1980.

Barry Carse

MS *Saint Columba*, 7836 grt, built in Denmark in 1976-7 for British Rail/Sealink's Holyhead-Dun Laoghaire service. The picture was taken in April 1977, probably on the occasion of the new ro-ro vessel's first arrival at Dun Laoghaire. In later years, when under the ownership of Stena Line, *Saint Columba* was renamed, first *Stena Hibernia* and later (and regrettably) *Stena Adventurer*. During her BR/Sealink days this ship was regarded as the flagship of the Irish Sea Fleet. In this view the railway branch to the harbour has been lifted – compare with page 27.

Derek Young

The Burns and Laird motor ship, *Royal Scotsman*, alongside Donegall Quay, Belfast in 1963. *Royal Scotsman*, along with her sister *Royal Ulsterman*, was built by Harland and Wolff in 1936 and was of 3244 grt. The further vessel is one of the 1956 'Dukes' of British Rail's Heysham-Belfast service. This ship is in the pre Sealink livery of the British Rail ships with a buff/black funnel.

Laurence Liddle

The *Innisfallen* of 1947, pictured here at Fishguard. This City of Cork SP Co (B and I Line) vessel was the only Coast Lines standard ship not to have been built by Harland and Wolff; she was built by Dennys of Dumbarton. The photo was taken from the *Duke of Rothesay*, about to leave for Rosslare in August 1967.

Coast Lines' Services

Before we start to consider the companies and services of the Coast Lines group, it is appropriate that I should mention that, whilst the railway operated routes have (with one exception) been listed in geographical order from north to south, I have dealt with the Coast Lines' companies alphabetically, and in company, not route, order. I decided on this arrangement for two reasons: first, so that the pioneer units of the 'standard' vessels could be covered at the beginning of this section of our story and second, in order to be able to deal with the two most important of the many transfers of ships within the group in the correct chronological order.

The four main subsidiary companies of the Coast Lines combine, which provided passenger services between Britain and Ireland after the First World War, the location of their individual head offices and the routes on which each company operated, were as follows:

Belfast Steamship Company (Belfast)
Belfast-Liverpool

British and Irish Steam Packet Co (Dublin)
Dublin-Liverpool
Dublin-London (No passenger service after 1932)

City of Cork Steam Packet Co (Cork)
Cork-Fishguard
Cork-Liverpool

Burns and Laird Lines (Glasgow)
Glasgow-Belfast
Glasgow-Derry
Glasgow-Dublin
Derry-Heysham (No passenger service after 1933)
Dublin-Heysham. (Not after 1927)
Ardrossan-Belfast
Glasgow-West coast of Ireland
(No passengers after mid 1930s)

Minor passenger services, which had been operated by the Ayr Steamship Company and the Dundalk and Newry Steam Packet Company, did not survive after the incorporation of these firms into the combine. However, the services and relevant ships are briefly dealt with later in the narrative.

BELFAST STEAMSHIP COMPANY

The only passenger service which this concern operated, after 1919, was the regular nightly (Sundays excepted) connection between Belfast and Liverpool, which had existed for very many years. At the beginning of our period the regular vessels on the route were the three twin-screw reciprocating-engined steamships, *Graphic*, 1871 grt and *Heroic*, 1869 grt, each with dimensions of 320'x 41', and *Patriotic*, 2254 grt, 325'x 42'. Building dates were 1906 for the two

J McRoberts

The *Patriotic* of 1912, 2254 grt, 325′ x 42′, the largest and last built of the three regulars on the Belfast Steamship Company's Belfast-Liverpool service in the early years of the present century.

sisters and 1912 for *Patriotic*. There was a fourth ship, the 1627 grt *Classic* (ex *Magic*), which had been built as far back as 1893. This vessel was transferred to the City of Cork Steam Packet Company in 1927 and will be referred to in greater detail when we come to consider that concern.

The *Graphic*, *Heroic* and *Patriotic* were generally similar in appearance and internal arrangements but there was a major mechanical difference between the *Patriotic* and her two half sisters. Somewhat unusually, the two older vessels had quadruple expansion engines, whilst the *Patriotic* had the commoner triple type. (Here we may recall that the four LNWR express steamers of 1898-1902 had four cylinder triple expansion machinery, with two low pressure cylinders per engine.) The BSS Co ships had midship structures two decks high, extending to the full width of the hulls in the case of the lower decks, but with narrow open-side decks at the higher level. There were no raised forecastles, the only upstanding structures, forward of the midship houses, being the turtle-backed coamings to the companionways to the crews' quarters. First class accommodation, situated midships, comprised a dining saloon, a small lounge and sleeping cabins on the lower passenger deck and a smoke room/bar and more cabins on the upper. There was also a small semi-open public room on the after end of this deck which, during the ships' latter years at any rate, had the pretentious, not to say unapt (for a night service vessel), name of 'verandah café'. Third class passengers were housed at the after end of the ship, in the usual very basic quarters of the pre-1914 era. As always, however, these included a bar. The three ships, whose distinctive appearance was accentuated by their very tall single funnels, carried three boats on each side, two amidships and one aft.

It may be wondered why, with only one service each way every twenty four hours and none on Sundays, three regular ships and a standby (the *Classic*) were required, after the BSS Co, and other Irish Sea companies, had been merged into the Coast Lines Group. Surely a relief vessel could have been forthcoming from among the many craft of the Burns and Laird Lines, or perhaps a spare ship could have been shared between the BSS and B and I for their respective Liverpool services (This indeed became the case in the early 1950s). The reason that three ships were required to maintain the normal service, until after the end of the Second World War, was that, until 1950, the Liverpool dock (from memory the Nelson Dock), used by both the Belfast and the Dublin passenger ships, could be entered and left only within a certain number of hours on either side of high water. Consequently, if the tide did not permit immediate passage through the lock leading to the dock, when one of the Irish vessels arrived in the Mersey, passengers were disembarked at Princes landing stage, after which the ship anchored out in the river until conditions were right for her to proceed to her berth. With favourable tides the vessel would berth straightaway at the dockside. Comparable conditions, necessitating alternative places of embarkation, obtained for sailings from Liverpool. It was therefore necessary to have three ships in operation if a regular nightly service was to be maintained. Normal rostering was:

Ship A, ex-Belfast on Mondays and Thursdays and ex-Liverpool on Wednesdays and Saturdays;

Ship B, ex-Belfast on Tuesdays and Fridays and ex-Liverpool on Thursdays and Mondays;

Ship C, ex-Belfast on Wednedays and Saturdays and ex-Liverpool on Fridays and Tuesdays.

If required, a duplicate service from Liverpool could be provided by cancelling the overnight lie over of one vessel at that port, enabling it to return to Belfast, either immediately after arrival and disembarkation of passengers or later the same day. These procedures would allow the operation of a second service from Belfast, either that night, or during the following day. While such methods of operation were useful in providing for heavy holiday weekend traffic, they obviously restricted the amount of time available for loading and discharging cargo.

In 1929-30 the *Patriotic*, *Graphic* and *Heroic* were given major refits and transferred to the British and Irish Steam Packet Company. They were replaced by three new twin-screw motor ships, *Ulster Monarch* in 1929 and *Ulster Queen* and *Ulster Prince* in 1930, each of 3791 gross tons and with main dimensions of 346'x 46'. These vessels, which came from Harland and Wolff's Belfast yard,

World Ship Society

The *Ulster Prince*, built in 1930 by Harland and Wolff for the Belfast Steamship Company's Liverpool-Belfast service. This was one of the pioneer trio of a group of Coast Lines standard ships which eventually totalled thirteen vessels, all of basically similar design. Each of the three BSS Co ships was of 3791 grt and measured 346'x 46'.

were the first of a standard class of passenger/cargo motor-ship for Coast Lines' Irish services, of which thirteen were built between 1929 and 1957. With the introduction of the three 'Ulsters', the Belfast Steamship Company could justifiably claim to equal the railway companies' standards as regards both size of ships and passenger amenities.

The new Belfast vessels were of the 'three island' type, having raised forecastles, midship structures two decks high and one-deck-high poops. Cruiser sterns were standard and four boats per side were carried under gravity davits amidships. Propulsion was by Burmeister and Wain diesels, constructed under licence by Harland and Wolff. The new 'Ulsters' each had two short funnels, smaller versions of the type fitted by the builders to the almost contemporary *Carnarvon Castle*, *Winchester Castle*, *Reina del Pacifico*, *Britannic* and *Georgic*, to whose general outlines these cross-channel ships bore a striking resemblance.

The greater part of the accommodation in the midship structures was given over to single and two-berth first class sleeping cabins, including a number of 'Bibby Rooms'. These were arranged in such a way that what would otherwise have been an inside cabin with no natural lighting, had a portlight at the end of a narrow alleyway opening off one end of the room. Presumably the name for this type of sleeping accommodation was due to it having first been used on vessels of the Bibby Line, trading between Liverpool, Burma, the Straits Settlements (now part of Malaysia) and Singapore. Towards the after-end of the lower superstructure deck were the ship's bureau and a dining saloon, the galley being aft of the latter. This lower deck, which extended out to the full beam of the ship, was plated in for its entire length but the deck above had open-side decks for about the after quarter of its length, inboard of which was a first class lounge. The remainder of this deck was taken up with sleeping accommodation. Above again, on the boat deck, there was a long structure in which were situated a bar/smoking room aft and quarters for both deck and engineers officers forward. Third class accommodation, situated in the poop, was of a somewhat higher standard than had obtained in earlier vessels, comprising a general public room, bar, dining room and some multi-berth cabins.

The new ships had fairly extensive cargo space in holds and 'tween decks forward and aft of the midship structure, two fore-hatches and one after-hatch were served by derricks and electric winches, the latter an innovation on Coast Lines' Irish routes.

The foregoing description of the pioneer vessels of 1929-30 applies generally to all the other ten ships of the class although, as will be noted, there were differences of detail between individual vessels or pairs of vessels from 1931 onwards.

The BSS Co's new ships ran to much the same schedules as their predecessors had done and for which their speed of 17 knots was ample for the nine hour passage. An interesting diversion from the regular summer schedule of the *Ulster Prince*, during at least some of the 1930s, was the use of this ship to provide short weekend cruises from Liverpool to the west coast of Scotland. No calls were advertised and the turning point was the north end of the Sound of Mull.

From 1930 onwards, the Belfast Steamship Company was providing a passenger service which, so far as comfort and other amenities were concerned, was at least the equal of and, in the opinion of many travellers, superior to, that of the railway company on the Heysham route. The only clear advantage which the LMS could offer was that the overall time between Belfast and London, via Heysham, was shorter than that through Liverpool. However, where time was not of the essence, the more civilised arrival time at the Mersey port more than compensated for the 0530 caper at Heysham. Here it may be noted that, since there was no direct rail access for passengers to the BSS Liverpool berth, a 'free' bus service operated between the ship's side and the city's railway termini. I understand that, strictly speaking, this facility was available only for travellers holding through boat/rail tickets from places in Ireland to places in Britain and vice versa. However, in my experience of many journeys through Liverpool by both BSS Co and B and I Line routes, no one was ever asked to produce a through, or any other ticket, when boarding the bus. At Donegall Quay, Belfast, the arrangements for passengers via Liverpool were similar to those obtaining in the case of the Heysham route. One walked or took a taxi.

The 'Ulsters' were all involved in war service and the *Ulster Queen* was lost in the Mediterranean. The *Ulster Prince*, which had been requisitioned by the British Government on the outbreak of war, was converted for use as a naval auxiliary. The vessel survived the war but did not return to her owners. The

W Grogan

Ulster Monarch, 1929-1967, the first built and last survivor of the Belfast Steamship Company's three standard ships of the interwar years. The picture was taken after the vessel had had her post-war refit, as is evidenced by the streamlined funnels and the black hull.

D B McNeill

Ulster Prince, ex *Leinster*, built in 1937. This ship, which had a gross tonnage of 4302 and main dimensions of 353' x 58', was transferred to the BSS Co from the British and Irish section of Coast Lines after the Second World War.

Ulster Monarch, the eldest of the three, which served as an infantry landing ship, returned to the Belfast-Liverpool service, on which she remained until 1967. That year two new ro-ro vessels were placed on the route. During the post-war refit the *Ulster Monarch* was somewhat altered, and to my mind improved, in appearance, receiving two streamlined funnels and having the solid bulwarks on the boat deck replaced by rails. During the post-war period, this ship's consort was a newly named, though not new, *Ulster Prince*, which had been built in 1937 as the *Leinster* for the British and Irish Steam Packet Company's Dublin-Liverpool service.

I made a number of crossings in both the *Ulster Monarch* and the during the 1950s and 1960s. Looking back over a gap of thirty years, I have two abiding memories of the former vessel, one being the contrast between the 1920s style of interior decor (wood panelling in the bar for example) and the plastic fittings of post-war ships; the other a seemingly permanent slight list to port which the ship maintained, irrespective of weather conditions. I will have more to say about the *Ulster Prince* when we come to consider the B and I Line's ships.

For saloon passengers at any rate, Belfast-Liverpool was a very pleasant route by which to travel during the first two post-war decades. The ships were spotlessly clean both inside and on deck, the catering facilities were good and, even though by 1960 the *Ulster Monarch* was thirty-one years old and the *Ulster Prince* twenty-three, their general accommodation, and particularly the sleeping facilities, were comfortable and mostly well ventilated. I say mostly, because there was an occasion, on a hot July night in 1951, when my wife and I, and our two young sons, had a somewhat less than ideal crossing in a 'tween deck four-berth cabin in the *Ulster Monarch* — however that was exceptional.

What a leisurely and relaxed way of travel an overnight passage from Belfast was in those days, compared to a journey through Stranraer, Dun Laoghaire or Rosslare today. There was ample time to board the vessel and have a meal before sailing. There were restaurant facilities with waiter service, compared to the current queuing at cafeteria counters for half cold fried food. There was no particular rush to disembark in the morning, a civilised breakfast was available and (a point which cannot be over-emphasised), with the ample lie-over time the ships had in each port and the absence of today's multiple crewing, there was real cleanliness everywhere. This was to a degree which a later generation, used only to ro-ro vessels with their dirty unkempt steel decks, and oil stained carpets on the companionways from car deck to passenger accommodation, may find hard to envisage. I am well aware of the economic factors which have led to the intensive use and multi-crewing of today's cross-channel vessels and I am aware, too, of the tendency of the elderly to view the past through rose coloured spectacles. Nevertheless, for those who (or whose employers) were prepared to pay saloon fares, a cross-channel passage in the 1950s, or early 1960s, was a vastly different, and infinitely more civilised, experience than anything available today, whether one travelled in a Coast Lines 'standard' ship, on any of the routes on which these vessels operated, or in a railway owned steamer.

The *Ulster Monarch* and *Ulster Prince* were replaced in 1967 by two new ro-ro ships, *Ulster Queen* and *Ulster Prince* which, however, had relatively short lives with the Belfast Steamship Company, due partly to their unsuitability for a comprehensive ro-ro service — they had stern loading only and inadequate accommodation for freight vehicles — and partly to the growing tendency for traffic across the Irish Sea to concentrate on the short sea routes. Before the new *Ulster Queen* and *Ulster Prince* took up service, however, two newcomers put in occasional spells between Belfast and Liverpool. These were the standard vessels *Irish Coast* of 1953 and *Scottish Coast*, which was built in 1957, with main dimensions and tonnages of 339'8"x 51'7" and 3813 grt, for the former, and 342'3"x 52'8" and 3817 grt, for the latter.

For the first four years of her career, the *Irish Coast*, registered in Liverpool as owned by Coast Lines, was operated as a general relief vessel for all four subsidiary sections of the combine: Belfast Steamship; British and Irish; Burns and Laird and City of Cork, standing in for each of the other seven standard vessels when these were withdrawn for annual survey, which usually lasted for about a month for each ship. During the summer season the *Irish Coast* operated the 'daylight' Belfast-Ardrossan service of the Burns and Laird Line. In her later years the *Irish Coast* became the regular passenger vessel on the same company's Dublin-Glasgow route, whilst the *Scottish Coast* succeeded her as the general relief ship and also worked the Ardrossan summer service. The *Irish Coast* was similar in all main respects to earlier standard ships. The only immediately noticeable feature in which she was unique was that throughout her Irish Sea career, and irrespective of what subsidiary company's service she might be operating, her single funnel was painted in the black with large white 'V' of Coast Lines. So far as I can remember, I made only two passages in the *Irish Coast* but they are worth recalling, as exemplifying the diverse nature of her employment. The first of these crossings was between Dublin and Liverpool and the second from Belfast to Ardrossan.

The *Scottish Coast*, which was almost a mirror image of her sister, differed from her in sporting a funnel painted in the standard later day colours of the Burns and Laird Line and the Belfast Steamship Company, red with black top, beneath which was a narrow blue line. She was registered in Liverpool, but in the name of Burns and Laird. During the later 1960s, a mechanical lift arrangement was installed on the quaysides at Belfast and Ardrossan, by which side loading and unloading of cars to the fore well deck (and thence to the 'tween deck) of the *Scottish Coast*, could be effected. As was the case with her elder sister, this vessel provided me with examples of her versatility. I have travelled in her between Liverpool and Belfast and between Belfast and Glasgow.

My latest recollection of the Belfast-Liverpool route dates from the spring of 1970. When one of the new ro-ro ships was withdrawn for survey, the replacement vessel was the *Saint Clair* (the third of the name) of the erstwhile North of Scotland and Orkney and Shetland Shipping Company, which concern had recently been acquired by Coast Lines. The *Saint Clair*, 297′x 49′ and of 3302 grt, was a twin-screw diesel-engined vessel, which had been built in 1960 for the Aberdeen-Lerwick direct service of the 'North Company', as it was commonly called. She was an excellent vessel for the route for which she had been designed, (I made one passage in her, to Lerwick in 1969), but as a ro-ro replacement she was far from ideal, since all vehicles had to be craned on and off the ship.

This substitution of a conventional, for a ro-ro, vessel, even if only for a short time and on a service which had for some time been losing traffic to the Stranraer route, has always seemed to me to be symptomatic of how out of touch Coast Lines had become with the rapidly changing requirements of the travellers of the late 1960s. Another example of this remoteness was the almost unchanged nature of the steerage accommodation of the *Irish Coast* and *Scottish Coast* from that of the 'Ulsters' of a quarter of a century earlier. A whole generation and a world war had intervened between the building of the two groups of vessels, but still the 'thirds' were packed into the most vibration prone part of the ship and still, in the summer season, some of these travellers were accommodated also in a most primitive manner in the 'tween decks, an area usually reserved for cattle. It is, however, only fair to say that, in the three original 'Ulsters', livestock were not carried in this area. Pleasant enough as they were for first class passengers to travel in, the 1953 and 1957 'Coasts' compared very badly with the 1956 'Dukes', and even the *Saint Patrick* and *Saint David* of 1947 and 1948, so far as third class facilities were concerned.

Finally, to return for a moment to the *Saint Clair* being used on the Belfast-Liverpool route in 1970, by this year there would have been little difficulty in chartering a ro-ro ship outside the peak of the holiday season, either from Sealink or from a Continental European company. Nevertheless, as the last conventional passenger ship to operate between Belfast and Liverpool the *Saint Clair* deserves to be remembered. Ironically, by 1970, this vessel herself, though only ten years old, was an anachronism and was replaced by a ro-ro vessel in 1972, by which time what was left of Coast Lines had been acquired by P and O.

THE BRITISH AND IRISH STEAM PACKET COMPANY

Traditionally the primary passenger service of the old established British and Irish Line had been between Dublin and London, with calls at Plymouth and Southampton. From the end of the First World War, until 1933, five ships were employed on the London route, though only two — the *Lady Wimborne*, 1542 grt, 260′x 38′, built in 1915 and the *Lady Cloë*, 1581 grt and with the same overall dimensions as the *Lady Wimborne*, but dating from 1916 — carried passengers. These two ships provided first class accommodation only, at a Dublin-London single fare of £5, exclusive of the cost of meals. In pre-First World War days the *Lady Roberts*, *Lady Hudson-Kinahan*, and other craft, had catered for steerage passengers as well as for those travelling 'saloon'.

The *Lady Wimborne* and the *Lady Cloë* usually had their passenger accommodation well filled during the summer months of the 1920s and early 1930s. In the years before long distance holiday travel was common, to go to and from London by 'long sea' was considered by many to be a treat in itself. How many people made the trip in winter and, of those, how many expended much money over and above the basic £5, is probably another story. Apart altogether from what the weather, in the darker days of the year, might be expected to offer 'long sea' voyagers, the price difference — about £3 for a 'saloon boat, third rail' return between London and Dublin via Liverpool, as compared to the aforesaid £5 single — ensured that, whatever may have been the case for steerage passengers before 1914, only afficionados used the *Lady Cloë* and *Lady Wimborne* during the winters of the later years of the service.

These two ships on the London route were conventional three-island steamships, with two hatches forward of the midship structure and one aft. This structure was two decks high. The lower, extending to the full beam of the vessel, was plated in, whilst the upper had open alleyways on each side. Motive power for the single screw was a three cylinder triple-expansion engine. Although I often saw these vessels at their berth at Sir John Rogerson's Quay in Dublin during my teenage dockside saunterings, neither I, nor any member of my family, ever travelled in either of them and so I am unable to describe their accommodation.

In 1933 due to a combination of the world-wide trade depression, a considerable increase in tariff protection for Irish industries and the opening of the new Guinness brewery at Park Royal, London, there were major changes in the Dublin-London service of the B and I and also in the operations of two other Coast Lines companies. So far as the *Lady Cloë* and the *Lady Wimborne* were concerned, these ships now called at Cork on some sailings and also at Le Havre, thereby eliminating the separate Cork-London service of the City of Cork Steam Packet Co and the cargo-only service between Dublin and northern France (Le Havre, Boulogne and Dunkirk), which had been operated by the Dublin firm of Michael Murphy and Company, a minor member of the Coast Lines group. This concern had also served Bristol Channel ports from Dublin, a route which, from 1933, was reduced to occasional calls at Cardiff by the Dublin-London ships of the B and I. A personal note — the only Michael Murphy ship which I remember seeing was the *Finola*, a cargo vessel of 879 grt, which dated from 1920.

After 1933 the *Lady Cloë* and the *Lady Wimborne* continued to operate for a while under the aegis of the British and Irish, though without passenger certificates. In 1938, however, these vessels were absorbed into the directly-owned Coast Lines fleet, the *Lady Cloë* becoming the *Normandy Coast* whilst her sister, after a short spell as the B and I *Galway*, became the *Galway Coast*. The Dublin to London service was eventually amalgamated with the Liverpool-London connection, provided by the parent company under its own name. This route survived until about the mid 1950s. Towards the end it was operated by diesel-engined cargo vessels with accomodation for twelve passengers.

I have already referred to the City of Dublin Steam Packet Company and its

W Grogan

Galway Coast, built in 1915 for the British and Irish Steam Packet Company's Dublin-London service as the *Lady Wimborne*. She was of 1542 grt and measured 260'8"x 38'. The photo dates from some time after 1933 when the vessel was operating for Coast Lines, although she still retains her B and I funnel colours.

J McRoberts

An early photograph of the long lived steamship *Wicklow* (later *Lady Wicklow* and then again *Wicklow*), which was built for the City of Dublin Steam Packet Company in 1895. The *Wicklow*, 1174 grt, 260'8"x 34', passed to the British and Irish section of Coast Lines, when the B and I absorbed the remains of the City of Dublin company soon after the end of the First World War.

operation of the mail service between Dun Laoghaire (then known as Kingstown) and Holyhead until just after the end of the First World War. Other routes, on which the City of Dublin had run passenger ships, had been between Dublin and Liverpool/Manchester and Dublin and Belfast. The latter service did not survive but the former, as between Dublin and Liverpool and incorporating the service formerly provided by the Dublin firm of Tedcastle McCormick and Company between the same two ports, became, under B and I auspices, a popular alternative to the Holyhead route.

After the incorporation of the City of Dublin Company in the B and I, the Dublin-Manchester service continued to operate for general cargo, with calls at Birkenhead to land livestock from Ireland. One of the erstwhile passenger vessels on the route, the *Wicklow*, later *Lady Wicklow* and then again *Wicklow*, but without a passenger certificate, continued to run under B and I ownership, and mostly on the Manchester route, until 1946, even though she had been built as far back as 1895. This vessel was of 1174 grt, with main dimensions of 260'x 34'. The *Wicklow* name was perpetuated by other British and Irish cargo vessels. The last of these, a container ship, was disposed of in 1994.

As the operation of the Holyhead mail service by the City of Dublin company ceased just after the end of the First World War, it hardly qualifies to be dealt with at any length here. It is worth remembering, however, that the scheduled port to port times of the twin screw *Ulster*, *Munster*, *Leinster* and *Connaught*, built

Sean Kennedy/Green studios

The City of Dublin Steam Packet Company's mail steamer *Connaught*, built in 1896, alongside the arrival side of Dun Laoghaire (then known as Kingstown) mail boat pier. This long remembered ship was of 2645 grt and measured 360'8"x 41'. She was one of the casualties of the First World War. Note the crew's washing hung out to dry above the turtle back forecastle. The strange looking craft in the foreground is the harbour authorities' diving boat.

in 1896, with gross tonnages of between 2640 and 2650 and hull dimensions of 360'x 41', were not surpassed during the inter-war years, even though the LNWR ships of 1920-21 were capable of somewhat higher maximum speeds. Just as those railway steamers were the most outstanding cross-channel vessels of the 1919-1939 period, so their CDSP Co predecessors marked the peak of achievement in the days of the reciprocating steam engine. Two of these fine Irish vessels became war victims, the *Connaught* on Government service, and the *Leinster* on passage Dun Laoghaire-Holyhead in the autumn of 1918.

This latter loss, doubly tragic in that it occurred only just before the end of the war, was due to a torpedo from a German submarine a short distance to the east of the Kish Bank lightship, less than half an hour's steaming from Dun Laoghaire. The heavy loss of life ensured that the tragedy is still remembered in Ireland.

I have mentioned that one of my early memories, from an Irish Sea crossing, is of travelling from Holyhead in the railway steamer *Curraghmore*. Two even earlier recollections relate to the CDSP Co. The first of these is that I have always had a memory of being in a large open cabin with my mother and that in the

Laurence Liddle

The coat of arms of the City of Dublin Steam Packet Co, still preserved on the face of the building on Eden Quay Dublin, which housed the company's offices.

Laurence Liddle

One of the anchors of the CDSP Co's *Leinster*, 1896-1918. This ship was torpedoed off the Kish lightship at the outer approaches to Dublin Bay, about one month before the end of the First World War. The anchor has been raised from the wreck and is on permanent display near the landward end of Carlisle Pier (the Mail boat pier) Dun Laoghaire. The *Leinster* was a twin of the *Connaught* shown opposite.

centre of this apartment there was an arrangement of white pipes and a large wheel. Imagine my gratification some years ago when, as I was examining an accommodation plan of the City of Dublin mail steamers, I found that a pump (presumably a manually operated standby apparatus) was shown as being situated in the first class ladies' cabin. At the age of just three years, early in 1918 I was still eligible for entry to that arcane apartment.

My second City of Dublin memory, though not relating to an actual crossing, dates from later in the same year as that of the pump episode and is of my father, who was reading a newspaper, looking up and saying "The *Leinster* has sunk". Need I remind younger readers that in those days there was no radio, let alone television, news?

I last saw the old mail boats after the withdrawal of the two survivors *Munster* and *Ulster*. The pair were lying at moorings in the outer harbour at Holyhead. My father pointed them out to me at the end of a daylight crossing from Dun Laoghaire in one of the railway ships.

The City of Dublin Steam Packet Company, founded in the very early years of steam navigation, has been gone for more than seven decades but at least three reminders of it still exist. The first is a relief of the company's coat of arms on the face of the building at the corner of Eden Quay and Marlborough Street, Dublin, which once housed the company's offices. The second is a half model of the *Leinster* in the Irish National Maritime Museum, Dun Laoghaire, just three minutes walk from the Carlisle Pier, from which this ship and her three sisters, with their black hulls and funnels and long turtle-backed forecastles under which forty postal sorters worked, maintained for twenty years the fastest and most prestigious cross-channel service in Europe. The third reminder is an anchor recently raised from the wreck of the *Leinster*, which is on permanent display on the sea front at Dun Laoghaire, close to the Carlisle pier.

To return to the British and Irish, we have seen that Tedcastle McCormick and Co ran a passenger service between Dublin and Liverpool. This firm, which still nominally exists, though no longer as shipowners, was primarily interested in the coal trade between Britain and Ireland and, at the end of the First World War, owned a number of small colliers and general cargo vessels, all dating from the 1890s or early 1900s, none of which need concern us here.

However, the company had one modern passenger vessel, the *Killiney*, 1166 grt, 250'x 36', built in 1918 and which, on the takeover of the Tedcastle fleet by the B and I, became the *Lady Killiney*. This vessel, of conventional three island type and with the standard arrangement of two forward and one after hatches, had a long fully-plated-in midship structure with a small deck house above this, immediately below the bridge, which gave access to the saloon accommodation. Third class passenger facilities were in the stern, where there were a deck house and open side decks. The *Lady Killiney*, together with the *Lady Kildare*, 1217 grt, 245'x 44'1", which dated from 1920 and had started life as G and J Burns's *Setter*, presumably continued in the Dublin-Liverpool service until the advent of the new ships shortly to be described. I use the word 'presumably' because I never knew the *Lady Killiney* until the 1930s, nor can I remember anything about the Liverpool passenger service before 1923. In this year, the *Lady Killiney* was transferred to the City of Cork Steam Packet Company and became the *Ardmore*, although the *Lady Kildare* remained with the B and I for a few more years. She eventually went to the Belfast Steamship Company and ended her days as the cargo/livestock vessel *Ulster Castle*. The *Ardmore* (ex *Lady Killiney*) was stripped of her passenger accommodation in the 1930s and had her funnel colours changed back, from the white with black top of the CCSP Co, to the green with black top of the British and Irish, though she retained her Cork registration. She operated on various B and I and CCSP cargo and livestock routes until she was lost, with all hands, on passage Cork-Fishguard during the Second World War. Only one body, that of the master, was ever found — on a Welsh beach, about a week after the tragedy. It is thought that a mine was responsible for the sinking.

The B and I Line acquired three ships for the improved service between Dublin and Liverpool, the *Lady Longford*, *Lady Louth* and *Lady Limerick*, two of which were destined to have long lives in Coast Lines service. These three vessels were very similar in external appearance and varied only slightly in main dimensions, though there were differences in gross tonnages and building dates. The *Lady Louth* and *Lady Limerick* came to the B and I directly from the builders — the Ardrossan Dockyard Company — which, like Coast Lines, was a member of the Royal Mail group. Delivery dates were 1923 for the *Lady Louth* and 1924 for her sister. The *Lady Longford*, also built at Ardrossan, had started life in 1921 as the City of Cork's *Ardmore*. Her gross tonnage, on dimensions of 274'x 38', was 1776, whilst the other two ships, which measured 277'x 38', had gross tonnages of 1870 (*Lady Louth*) and 1945 (*Lady Limerick*). The latter two ships had a distinctive square and solid appearance, with virtually no sheer, upright masts and single funnels. My recollection of the *Lady Longford* and of her sister the *Kenmare* is that they were less chunky looking. Each of the trio had a substantial cargo and livestock capacity and, though they were by no means fast, ample speed for the eight-nine hour, one hundred and twenty mile crossing. The improved Liverpool service was advertised as 'The Comfort Route'. A shorter passage time would have resulted in travellers having less than a reasonable night's sleep. As things were, the only constant factor likely to result in unduly early awakening was the discharging of cattle at Birkenhead, before arrival at Liverpool. However the *Lady Longford*, *Lady Louth* and *Lady Limerick* were steady and comfortable ships, which soon became justly popular with travellers.

The new 'Ladies' were of the three island type with raised forecastles, forward and after-well decks, two deck high midship structures and after-deck houses, inboard of open side-decks. The lower of the two midship decks was plated in but the upper had narrow open alleyways which, though sometimes referred to as 'promenade decks', scarcely merited that title. Three boats per side were carried amidships in quadrant davits, together with one per side under rotary davits on the poop house. Counter sterns were rather old fashioned for the 1920s but oil firing was rare for an Irish Sea passenger ship at the time. Free standing steam cranes, rather than the conventional derricks and winches, were used for cargo handling at the two forward and one after hatches. Freight could be carried in the holds, and in the upper and lower 'tween decks, though the two latter spaces were, on sailings from Dublin, largely used to accommodate livestock.

In the new 'Ladies', first class facilities comprised a dining saloon, right forward in the lower deck of the midship structure, aft of which apartment were sleeping cabins, and a general public room, forward on the so called 'promenade deck', with more cabins aft of this. In the *Lady Louth* and the *Lady Limerick* there were, so far as I remember, small semi-open shelters right aft on the promenade deck. In the *Lady Longford* certainly, and in the other two ships probably (though here my memory is not too clear), additional sleeping berths could be made up in the dining saloon. Admonitory notices, which were prominently displayed on the boat and promenade decks, stated, "Passengers are reminded that noise created by walking and talking on deck, after eleven pm, is disturbing to those who have retired to their cabins." As was normal at the time, third class accommodation was spartan, and not enhanced by proximity to the livestock pens.

The B and I Dublin-Liverpool service operated six nights per week in each direction and in its main features paralleled the BSS Co's service from Belfast to the Mersey. The need to use three vessels, provision of buses to and from the Liverpool railway termini and rail connections to and from these stations, were the same for each company. At North Wall Quay, Dublin, which had no direct rail connection to the B and I berths, the company provided a bus service from and to Kingsbridge (now Heuston) terminus, though not to any of the city's other stations. Through single and return tickets, between places in Ireland and those in Britain, were available by B and I ship, via Liverpool, or by the LMS Holyhead steamers. This was subject to the payment of a small supplement, if tickets routed through Liverpool were used via Holyhead. (No reduction was available the other way round.) Comparable arrangements were in force between the Belfast Steamship Company and the LMS on their Liverpool and Heysham services respectively. Port to port tickets issued for any of the Coast Lines' Irish routes were available on any of the others, subject in certain cases to payment of an excess fare.

Finally, as regards the three 'Ladies' of 1921/24, and on a personal note, the *Lady Limerick* was the first B and I, though not the first Coast Lines, vessel on which I travelled. The occasion was the return from Belgium, via England, of a school party in the Easter holidays of 1929. (The outward journey was made via Holyhead.)

Steadily growing popularity of the Dublin-Liverpool service soon led to a need for larger ships, a need which was filled, in the common Coast Lines manner, by a transfer of vessels between subsidiary companies. In this case the *Patriotic*, *Heroic* and *Graphic* were, on the introduction of the 'Ulster' motor ships, given extensive overhauls and became the *Lady Leinster*, *Lady Munster* and *Lady Connaught* respectively. The overhauls embraced other changes than those of

World Ship Society

The erstwhile *Graphic* of the Belfast Steamship Company after she had been extensively refitted and transferred to the British and Irish Steam Packet Company as *Lady Connaught*. Note the twin motor ship funnels which replaced the original tall single smokestack. The ship was renamed *Longford* in 1938.

World Ship Society

The *Lady Munster*, ex *Heroic*, built in 1906 for the Belfast Steamship Company and transferred to the British and Irish Steam Packet Company in 1930, was a sister ship to the *Graphic / Lady Connaught / Longford*. The vessel was renamed *Louth* in 1938 and, after the Second World War, by which time she had returned to the Belfast Steamship Company, she became the *Ulster Duke*.

name, funnel colours and port of registry. The tall single smokestacks were removed and replaced by short twin 'motor-ship' erections and, more importantly, oil replaced coal as fuel.

When I saw a picture of one of the renovated ships on an advertising poster on a Dublin suburban railway station, before I actually encountered one of these newcomers to the B and I, I was puzzled. I knew that short twin funnels were the latest fashion, particularly for motor vessels, but these did not tie in with rotary davits or counter sterns, both of which features were apparent in the picture. Even at the age of fifteen, and before seeing one of them, I realised that these were not new ships and that at least some of the fulsome information printed below the picture represented a certain economy with the truth. However, despite a somewhat less than convincing face-lift, the three vessels became popular with travellers and continued to give service in one guise or another for many years.

As soon as the former Belfast craft took up duty in Dublin, the *Lady Limerick*, *Lady Louth* and *Lady Longford* became the Burns and Laird Lines' *Lairdscastle*, *Lairdsburn* and *Lairdshill*, under which names they will be further mentioned, when we come to consider the Scottish company's services.

In 1937 Harland and Wolff launched two standard passenger ships for the B and I. Named *Leinster* and *Munster*, these were improved versions of the 'Ulsters' of seven years previously. Internal arrangements and motive power were generally similar to those of the earlier vessels, but there were differences in outward appearance. One large pear-shaped funnel took the place of the two squat ones, whilst the hull colour was no longer the black or grey of earlier ships but was a light straw shade. An innovation for British and Irish vessels was the dropping of the 'Lady' prefix to their names. B and I vessels had been 'Ladies' from early days, though usually personal names were used, as exemplified by the *Lady Cloë* and *Lady Wimborne*. (Lady Wimborne was the wife of one of the later Lords Lieutenant of Ireland, in the days of British rule). When the City of Dublin Steam Packet Company, which used Irish geographical names, was taken over by the British and Irish the naming procedures were combined — hence *Lady Limerick*, *Lady Louth* and others.

To return to the new *Leinster* and *Munster*, a further small change in B and I practice, inaugurated by these ships, was that the funnel colours of green with black top were augmented by a narrow white band immediately below the black. The *Leinster* carried Belfast Steamship Company colours for a short while after she entered service. She was completed earlier than her consort and, at the end of 1937, ran briefly between Belfast and Liverpool. One evening that year, I was travelling by the Burns and Laird direct Belfast to Glasgow service and observed the *Leinster* in Harland's fitting out basin, looking every inch a BSS ship (only the name was a bit anomalous). The thought, no doubt unworthy, struck me that, perhaps for a second time in less than a decade, we in Dublin were going to be fobbed off with Belfast's leavings; albeit the *Ulster Monarch* and consorts would have been a great improvement on the face-lifted *Patriotic* and her sisters. However the *Leinster*'s borrowed plumage did not last long and, early in 1938, she and the *Munster* took up service on the route for which they had been built.

The gross tonnage of the *Leinster* was 4302 and of the *Munster* 4305, main dimensions in each case being 353′x 50′8″. These figures were slightly greater than those of the 'Ulsters'. Although both of the new vessels were registered in Dublin, the *Leinster* appeared in Lloyds' Register as being owned by Coast Lines, rather than by the B and I Company. It seems likely that emphasis on direct ownership of one of the vessels by the parent company, rather than through the Irish subsidiary, was connected with negotiations, begun in 1936, which were aimed at the British and Irish and the City of Cork concerns becoming independent of Coast Lines. In the event these negotiations did not bring about a complete severance, the only immediately apparent result being that henceforward the Cork ships were registered under British and Irish ownership. During the short period that the *Leinster* was operated by the Belfast Steamship Company, she was registered in Liverpool.

At the beginning of the Second World War, the *Leinster* went back to Liverpool registry and, after being requisitioned by the British Government as a troop carrier, served in that capacity for the duration of hostilities. When she returned to peacetime work she went to the BSS Co (this time permanently) as the *Ulster Prince* and, as already mentioned, ran along with the *Ulster Monarch* of 1929, on the Belfast-Liverpool route. In 1968 the *Leinster* (*Ulster Prince*) went to Epirotiki Lines of Greece, under whose ownership she became the *Adria*. I have heard, from more than one professional source, that this ship was reckoned to have been the best of all the thirteen standard motor vessels of the Coast Lines group. Certainly, I remember her in 1950s and 1960s as a comfortable and well appointed ship. Although in these two decades I always preferred, purely from historical interest, to travel between Belfast and Liverpool in the *Ulster Monarch*, there is no doubt that the *Ulster Prince* was the favourite of most regular travellers.

Early in 1940 the *Munster* which, together with the *Leinster*, had spent the very early months of the war laid up (owing to a dispute between crews and management over 'war risk' pay), was transferred to the Belfast-Liverpool route, though still under B and I ownership and with her Dublin, and hence neutral, registration. However, not long after this move, the ship was lost through striking a mine in the outer approaches to Liverpool.

The *Leinster* and *Munster* of 1937 were replaced on the B and I's Liverpool service in 1948, by two standard ships bearing the same names, which carried on the service until they, in their turn, were succeeded by two ro-ro vessels (again a *Munster* and a *Leinster*) in 1968 and 1969. There is an exhibition model of the 1948 *Leinster* in the Irish National Maritime Museum. The British and Irish Company perpetuated the names *Leinster* and *Munster* until 1993 when, no doubt as a public relations gimmick aimed at the tourist trade, the names *Isle of Innisfree* and *Isle of Innismore* were substituted. Whatever about publicity value,

World Ship Society

The *Louth*, ex *Lady Munster*, ex *Heroic*, built in 1906 for the Belfast Steamship Company's Belfast-Liverpool service. Note the post 1936 funnel markings of the British and Irish Steam Packet Co. The *Heroic/Lady Munster* and *Graphic/Lady Connaught* each measured 320'8"x 41'. Gross tonnage of the former, as built, was 1869 and of her sister, 1871.

historically this change can only be deplored. There had been 'Leinsters' and 'Munsters' operating between Ireland and Britain at least as far back as the 1860s, when the City of Dublin Company introduced four express paddle steamers, named after the four provinces, on the Dun Laoghaire-Holyhead mail service. At least Stena Sealink, as successors to the LNWR and LMS railways, kept, until recently, the equally historic names 'Hibernia' and 'Cambria', albeit with the prefix 'Stena' in each case.

When the new *Leinster* and *Munster* entered service, early in 1938, the old *Lady Munster* (ex-*Heroic*) and *Lady Connaught* (ex-*Graphic*) became surplus to immediate requirements but were retained in the nominal ownership of the B and I, under the names of *Louth* and *Longford* respectively. The ships were advertised to run between Liverpool and Glasgow, during the exhibition in the latter city, in 1938. Otherwise, they seem to have done little work over the remaining peacetime period, although they were available for relief duties on the Belfast-Liverpool and Dublin-Liverpool routes as required. From 1939 until 1945, still ostensibly B and I vessels, though registered in Liverpool, they were variously employed. Towards the end of the war the *Louth* ran opposite to the LMSR's *Cambria* on the Belfast-Heysham route, whilst the *Longford*, which earlier had been back on the Dublin-Liverpool service, relived her early days between Liverpool and Belfast. The only times I ever travelled in the *Louth*, under any of her four names, was when she was operating to and from

World Ship Society

Longford, ex *Lady Connaught*, ex *Graphic*, built for the BSS Co in 1906. Here we see this many-named and long lived vessel in her final form. Unlike her two running mates of many years, the *Longford*, after her transfer from her original owners in 1930, remained a British and Irish vessel for the rest of her life. She was sold for scrap in 1953.

Heysham. I well remember one sailing from that north Lancashire port in the summer of 1945 when, as was almost invariably the case at the time, the ship was carrying her full complement of passengers. I spent the night on the boat deck. Even though it was July, the air was cool enough and I counted myself lucky to be able to sit on the deck, with my back against a warm funnel.

After the war the *Louth* was renamed yet again, this time as *Ulster Duke*, and went back to her original owners, the Belfast Steamship Company. She ran between Belfast and Liverpool along with the *Leinster*/*Ulster Prince* and the *Ulster Monarch*, until 1950, when the provision of twenty-four hour access to Princes Dock, at the English port, enabled the service at last to be operated by two ships. The old vessel was withdrawn and, shortly afterwards, foundered while under tow to a Spanish shipbreaker's yard, an ignominious end to a long and useful career.

With the coming of peace the *Graphic*/*Lady Connaught*/*Longford* returned to the Dublin-Liverpool service until 1950, after which time she was operated as a relief and extra vessel for both the British and Irish and the BSS Companies, until the advent of the *Irish Coast*, in 1953, led to her withdrawal for scrapping. She had served for forty-seven years, appreciably longer than either of her sisters. During the autumns of 1950/51/52, when she relieved the *Ulster Prince* and *Ulster Monarch* on the Belfast-Liverpool service, her bright green funnels provided a striking contrast to the row of red or buff stacks sported by the Burns and Laird, Belfast Steamship and British Rail vessels lined up at Donegall Quay, Belfast, during the days she spent in her old home port.

The third member of the original Belfast trio, the *Patriotic/Lady Leinster* was retained in B and I service after 1937, since a third ship was still needed to partner the two new motor vessels. The fact that in that year two, and not three, new ships were put into service by the B and I, is an indication that plans to provide continuous access to the Liverpool dock were in hand before the outbreak of war. The old ship was renamed *Lady Connaught*, though why the 'Lady' prefix was retained, when by now all other British and Irish vessels — cargo/livestock as well as passenger — had lost it, I do not know. During the war the *Lady Connaught*, registered in Liverpool, served at various times on both the Dublin and the Belfast routes. Subsequently, after striking a mine, which caused serious damage, she was repaired and returned to service as a livestock carrier ,until the end of the war. She was refitted as a cruising vessel in 1946, after which treatment, and adorned with a single large streamlined funnel painted in Coast Lines fashion and under the name of *Lady Killarney*, she reinaugurated the parent company's summer cruises to the west coast of Scotland and the Western Isles. This service did not last long and the old *Patriotic* was scrapped in 1957.

The 'conventional' passenger service between Dublin and Liverpool was phased out during the years 1968 and 1969, the new ro-ro *Munster* taking up duty in the former year and her slightly larger sister *Leinster* during the

H S Corran/Epirotiki Lines

The B and I's standard motor ship *Munster*, 4142 grt, 366'10"x 50'2", built in 1948 and sold to Greek buyers twenty years later. After a comprehensive refit which somewhat altered her external appearance, she served as the cruise vessel *Orpheus* until 1994. This picture shows her in her later years when under the ownership of Epirotiki Lines.

following summer. The *Munster* of 1948 went to Epirotiki Lines and, as the *Orpheus*, continued in service as a cruising ship, in the eastern Mediterranean until 1994 and thus, so far as I know, outlasted all the other four post-war standard ships, all of which, like her, were sold to Mediterranean owners.

I did not travel in either of the 1948 B and I vessels as often as I did in the (ex *Leinster*) *Ulster Prince* or *Ulster Monarch*, since my many and regular cross channel journeys in the 1950s and 1960s were predominantly between Dun Laoghaire and Holyhead, or Belfast and Liverpool, with only occasional diversions to other routes. Such B and I journeys as I did make, during those decades, differed in no major respects from those in BSS Co vessels. The British and Irish Company, which was bought from Coast Lines by the Irish Government in the late 1960s, made a much more striking (and successful) change over to ro-ro operation than did its erstwhile sister concern, the Belfast Steam Company. On this latter and also because of the revolutionary nature of its new ships of 1968 and 1969, some mention should be made of the *Munster* and *Leinster* of those years.

The *Munster*, which was built in Germany by Werft Nobiskring of Rensburg, was bought off the peg by the B and I, who negotiated with the shipyard (and presumably with the company who had ordered the ship in the first place), to acquire the almost completed vessel. It seems that this unusual procedure was adopted because the Irish Government was anxious to develop the growing tourist trade by providing a ro-ro ship for the Dublin-Liverpool route as soon as possible. However, it was not only the *Munster* herself which was bought from the Germans, B and I ordered an improved version of the ship, to be named *Innisfallen*, from Nobiskring and acquired the rights for a sister ship – *Leinster* – to be built at the newly established Verolme shipyard in Cork.

The design of the *Munster* almost certainly owed something to the 'Viking' type of car ferry, as used originally by Townsend Thoresen, and also by Sealink in the case of *Earl William* and the very similar *Earl Harold*. The new *Munster* measured 110.22m x 18.09m and had a gross tonnage of 4067. Propulsion was by MAN diesels on twin screws. A bow thruster was fitted and, a novelty for an Irish Sea ship, the vessel was described as 'ice-strengthened'. As with all purpose built car carriers, the *Munster* had sleeping cabins (all of which, in her case, were two or four-berthed) below the car deck, reached by rather steep stairs. To digress for a moment for a personal reminiscence, in late 1972 my eighty-three year old mother, having successfully negotiated these stairs on a passage from Dublin to Liverpool, decided that once was enough and on the return journey preferred to sit up all night.

The capacity of the car deck could be maximised by using an auxiliary deck on the starboard side which could either be lowered to accommodate a second floor of cars, or raised to permit high commercial vehicles to be accommodated on the main deck. Above the car deck the forward end of the main passenger deck accommodated a cafeteria to starboard and a lounge with rows of reclining seats on the port side. Amidships were a shop, a children's playroom (later incorporated in the shop) and the purser's office. Aft of these were a large lounge, again fitted with reclining seats, and a bar. Above this main accommodation deck was the boat deck, at the fore end of which were a restaurant to starboard and a bar to port. Aft of these apartments was another lounge area with reclining seats, this latter apartment being designated a 'quiet area' on night crossings. Also on the boat deck were the galley and officers' dining room. Navigation bridge, wheelhouse and officers' accommodation were above the boat deck. Three boats per side were carried in gravity davits and there was a considerable amount of open space on the boat deck, since the accommodation at that level did not extend to the full length of the ship. Prominent features of the new vessel and her companion ships were a blue hull and a streamlined funnel painted in the traditional City of Cork SP Co's colours of white with a black top, on the fore end of which a short mast was stepped. On each side of the funnel a newly designed logo, in red, was carried.

As soon as the *Munster* took up duty on the Dublin-Liverpool route, her namesake of 1948 was sold to Mediterranean owners, as has already been recounted. At first the new ship ran opposite to the old *Leinster*, making one port to port passage each night but, very soon, traffic in cars and commercial vehicles developed sufficiently to justify the *Munster* making a return passage to Dublin-Liverpool each twenty-four hours. When the new *Leinster* became available in 1969, the Dublin-Liverpool route soon settled into a routine of a day and a night crossing each day, seven days per week. The usual schedule was for *Munster* to operate from Dublin at night and from Liverpool by day, with *Leinster* taking the opposite turns. To serve the ro-ro route, B and I established a new terminal at the seaward end of Dublin docks, some considerable distance from the old berth at North Wall. The Liverpool terminal was also changed although, after location at a temporary site, it was eventually established not far away from the earlier berth.

Leinster and *Innisfallen* (the latter built for a new Cork-Swansea service which will receive further mention in due course) were basically similar to *Munster* but slightly larger. These ships embodied some additions to the passenger accommodation; their gross tonnage and main dimensions were in each case 4849 and 118.19m x 17.84m. Each vessel was given a so-called 'sky lounge', built on top of the bridge and officers' quarters. This enabled the small lounge on the port side of the main accommodation deck to be incorporated in the cafeteria. The other principal addition to passenger facilities was that the large area of open boat deck at the after end of the quiet lounge was used to provide a number of two berth deck cabins. I never used any of these sleeping facilities, but they must have been a great improvement on the accommodation below the car deck. Despite my many decades of Irish Sea and other marine travel, and despite also my great liking for the sea and ships, I could never quite rid myself of a certain degree of claustrophobia in the cabins below the car deck, and usually preferred to use a reclining chair on the few night crossings I made in the 1968 *Munster* and 1969 *Leinster*. On the other hand, my wife and I travelled frequently on day sailings during the eleven and twelve years the ships were on the Liverpool route.

It will be seen that the one class passenger accommodation in these new ships was somewhat austere and utilitarian. It was not uncomfortable but, compared to the first class facilities of their predecessors, it was certainly unappealing. However, when compared to what third class travellers had to put up with in the earlier ships, it represented a great improvement . It is only fair to B and I to add that the standard of accommodation in the successors to *Munster* and *Leinster* – the *Connacht* of 1979 and the *Leinster* of 1980 – was very good.

Before we take leave of the *Munster,* I think that a bizarre occurrence in which the ship featured deserves to be recorded. After the sale of British Rail's Sealink services to private interests, the inner section of Holyhead harbour, hitherto the exclusive preserve of the railway vessels, became available to 'outside' users. This development was an attractive one to the B and I management, who almost immediately announced that, in future, their daylight service to and from Dublin would use Holyhead rather than Liverpool as its British terminal although, for the time being, the night route would continue to operate to and from Liverpool.

The prospect of the old enemy (the rivalry between the CDSP Co and the LNWR dated from the 1860s) entering their home territory was too much for Sealink staff and many of the general inhabitants of Holyhead, to swallow. No doubt, genuine fears for future employment, resulting from a possible co-ordination of services, had a lot to do with the reaction and, on arrival from Dublin, the first B and I vessel was prevented from berthing by a flotilla of local fishing boats and other small craft. There was nothing for the intruder to do but to withdraw.

The situation remained deadlocked for a day or two, but the B and I were not without means of retaliation. One spring evening, at the time of the impasse, I was returning from work by my usual train, on the Dublin and South Eastern suburban line. Approaching Dun Laoghaire station, I glanced out over the harbour, as I always did, and was somewhat surprised to see the *Munster,* which for the past couple of years had been chartered to a Scandinavian company operating between Norway and Denmark, apparently at anchor just off the harbour entrance. This phenomenon merited full investigation so, as soon as I had had my evening meal, I walked the two miles from my house down to the end of the east pier, where I was able to confirm that, not only was the *Munster* securely ensconced across the harbour mouth, but the *Saint David* (the 1981 ro-ro vessel) on the Holyhead Sealink service, was lying off about a mile away, unable to berth.

The next morning's newspapers informed us that the crew of the *Munster* which had been lying at North Wall Quay, Dublin, having just undergone her annual survey, had taken her across the bay and taken up station where I had seen her the previous evening. The B and I ship was still 'on station' as I made my way to work that morning but, by the evening, when I again surveyed the harbour from my homeward train, she had gone. It seems that a passenger in the

Saint David had been taken ill and that a request from the master of that ship to his opposite number in the *Munster*, to allow the Sealink vessel to enter harbour had been granted. That was the end of the affair, and the B and I service to Holyhead started to operate the next day. In due course the night passenger route to Liverpool was abandoned, enabling the British and Irish, now maintaining a twice daily service to and from Holyhead, to dispense with one of the two vessels hitherto employed.

With the question of access to the terminal ports settled, it was naturally not long before the thoughts of the management of the two companies turned towards effecting that rationalisation, the fear of which had been a major factor in the blockade of Holyhead. However, rationalisation was not to be. It was agreed between the companies that, on the withdrawal of the *Saint Columba* (the main Sealink vessel at Holyhead) for annual survey, the B and I *Leinster* (the 1980 Verlome-built successor to the 1966 vessel) should take over the double daily return sailings ex Dun Laoghaire and that the reverse process should apply when the *Leinster* went for survey. The *Leinster*'s officers refused to work the Sealink service unless their pay and conditions of employment were improved to equal those of their Sealink colleagues. B and I management refused to make any change and that was the end of any rationalisation. No doubt since the proposed arrangement would have operated during January and February, when traffic was slack and one ship could have accommodated all the passengers and vehicles travelling, it would have been economically helpful to both companies. However, from the point of view of those interested in ships per se, there were no regrets. Since each company had to provide relief vessels, from one of its other services in the case of Sealink, and by charter in the case of B and I, there was a greater variety of ships for us to see than would otherwise have been the case.

BURNS AND LAIRD LINES

The Burns and Laird Lines (generally referred to as the 'Burns Laird') which, during the 1930s, operated the greatest number of passenger services and owned the largest number of passenger vessels of the four main Coast Lines Irish Sea subsidiaries, inherited a very miscellaneous collection of ships from its two major constituent companies. A consequence of this situation was that, although the Glasgow-Belfast and Ardrossan-Belfast routes had their regular ships, matters were not so clear cut as regards the services to and from Dublin and Derry.

Until 1936, all the Burns Laird passenger vessels, with one exception, were single-screw steamships with reciprocating engines. The exception was the turbine steamer which operated the Ardrossan-Belfast summer-only daylight service. Apart from this latter craft, three basic patterns of passenger carrying ships were in use. I use the phrase 'passenger carrying' rather than 'passenger' deliberately. Burns Laird vessels were as important as freight and livestock carriers, as they were for passenger transport.

The oldest of the three types of ship comprised vessels of classic nineteenth century design, having their first class accommodation aft. This accommodation consisted of a dining saloon with fixed swivelling chairs (and in the oldest ships a single long table) and settees, together with a number of sleeping cabins most of which, other than the multi-berthed 'Ladies' ' and 'Gentlemens' ' apartments, were four-berthed. Both saloon and cabins were normally below 'promenade deck' level. Sometimes these ships had so called 'smoking rooms', small apartments either aft, incorporated in the saloon accommodation entrance, or on the midship boat deck, at the after end of the engine room skylight. There were rarely any other public rooms though, if the smoking room was on the boat deck, the space around the head of the companionway to the saloon quarters might be dignified by the name of 'lounge'. Berths could be, and at busy times were, made up in the public rooms. Third class passengers were very roughly catered for in the 'tween decks right forward, in close proximity to the livestock pens. These old ships had no below deck ventilation, other than what air came through the cowl ventilators unassisted by fan or blower. Their smell, compounded of cattle, coal smoke, vomit, metal polish, hot oil and cooking is not easily forgotten. The external appearance of the vessels was long and low with two masts and a single funnel. The engine and boiler room casings were flanked by narrow side decks, as was the deckhouse on the poop. Normally two boats per side were carried amidships and one aft. The holds were served by two forward and one after hatches.

The second type of ship had improved facilities for both classes of passenger. First class accommodation was amidships and third aft. The ships had fully-plated-in mid-ship superstructures extending to the full beam of the hull, in which were first class cabins and, at the fore end, the dining saloon. Above this midship section was a deckhouse below the bridge which, as has been mentioned in the case of the *Killiney* and the *Great Western*, contained the first class entrance. Here there was also usually a small lounge which, in the older vessels of the type, was little more than a space for a few armchairs at the head of the companionway. Some of the later vessels, however, had their lounge accommodation enlarged by glassing in the open decks at each side of this below bridge structure. An example of this feature can be seen in the picture of *Lairdsglen* on page 114. In a few ships, there was a very small smoking room/bar at the after end of the boat deck. Entrance to the third class space was in a poop house flanked by open side decks. On balance, this accommodation was probably less uncomfortable than what had been provided in the older vessels but it was to be some while yet before all ships had even multi-berth cabins for steerage passengers.

These ships of the second type, like their Victorian predecessors, carried three boats per side and had well decks fore and aft, with hinged bulwarks which opened flat against the ships' sides to facilitate the loading and unloading of livestock. I once saw a single decker bus being manhandled by a posse of dockers up a steep ramp of planks, which passed through an opening of this nature in a B and I cargo ship, when a low tide had resulted in the well deck level being appreciably below that of the quay. This second type of vessel was extensively used by the Clyde Shipping Company as well as by Burns and Laird. It probably reached its peak of development in the second *Saint Clair* of the North of Scotland Company, which entered service in 1937.

The third type of steamship to be found on Coast Lines services was a logical development of the second, in that a second deck was built above the basic midship structure, this deck having open sides throughout all, or most, of its length. Further comment on this design is unnecessary, as its features have been exemplified in what has already been said about the *Patriotic*, *Graphic* and *Heroic* and the 'Ladies' *Lady Limerick*, *Lady Louth* and *Lady Longford*. Even though the *Graphic* and *Heroic* dated from as far back as 1906, it was not until 1930 that the Burns Laird Line acquired any examples of this third pattern of ship. The *Lairdsrose*, ex *Rose*, of 1902, did not fully conform to the pattern of either type two or type three, as will be apparent from the photograph on page 113.

Before the fusion of the Burns and the Laird concerns, vessels of the former company had been named after animals or birds, whilst the Laird ships had carried tree or flower names. In 1930-31 all ships were renamed in a uniform style, with the prefix 'Lairds' in all cases. Funnels now became red with black tops, though for a while in the 1920s the smokestacks of the Burns ships had been painted in the erstwhile Laird colours of black top, red central section and white base. From 1936 onwards, a narrow blue band was added between the black and the red on all vessels. The house flag of the combined fleet was dark blue, on which was superimposed a heraldic lion in gold, which I think had been the Burns Line's flag. This flag closely resembled the Cunard house flag but with a blue, instead of a red, background. I have always assumed that this similarity of flags stemmed from the fact that the original George Burns of the Glasgow company was a partner of Samuel Cunard in the establishment of the Cunard company. While on the subject of house flags, that of the BSS Co was a red pennant, in the centre of which was a white star; whilst the B and I vessels flew white flags, on which were red and green superimposed crosses with the company's initials in the four quadrants.

In 1919 the main vessels of the Burns Company available for passenger service were as indicated below. I have used the expression 'main vessels' deliberately, since nearly all the ships of both the constituent companies had been built with some passenger accommodation, even though after the First World War this may have been rarely used in the smaller vessels.

G&J BURNS — PASSENGER SHIPS 1919

Hound	(1893)	1009 grt	250' x 32'	*Puma*	(1899)	1226 grt	265' x 35'
Pointer	(1896)	1153 grt	250' x 34'	*Tiger*	(1906)	1499 grt	275' x 37'
Vulture	(1898)	1246 grt	265' x 33'	*Partridge*	(1906)	1461 grt	276' x 36'
Magpie	(1898)	1247 grt	265' x 34'	*Woodcock*	(1906)	1470 grt	276' x 36'

None of these ships were young in 1919. However, in that year a new vessel, the *Killarney*, 1578 grt, 275′x 36′, was delivered to the City of Cork Steam Packet Company but, after a very short while as a member of that company's fleet, was transferred to G and J Burns, under whose ownership she became the *Moorfowl*. The Burns Line received its first brand new post-war vessel in 1920 when the *Setter*, 1217 grt, 245′x 34′, was delivered but, one year later, this ship went to the British and Irish as the *Lady Kildare*, under which name she has already been mentioned.

All of the above Burns ships, except the *Moorfowl*, *Puma*, *Tiger* and *Setter* were of the classic 'Victorian' type, with saloon accommodation aft. The four exceptions were all of the second type just described. The *Puma* and the *Tiger* had earlier in their careers belonged to the Dublin and Glasgow Sailing and Steam Packet Company, popularly known as 'the Duke Line', under whose ownership the vessels had been named *Duke of Rothesay* and *Duke of Montrose* respectively. Although G and J Burns absorbed the Duke Line they, presumably for accounting reasons, set up a subsidiary company under whose ownership

P & O

The Burns and Laird Lines' *Tiger*, later *Lairdsforest*, 1499 grt, 275′x 37′, built for the Duke Line's Dublin-Glasgow service, and originally named *Duke of Montrose*. The larger number of passengers in the photo suggest that at the time this was taken the *Tiger* may have been making a special excursion sailing. This vessel ended her days as the B and I Line's *Louth*.

these two vessels were registered.

The *Tiger* was the first ship of the Coast Lines combine in which I travelled — from Dublin to Glasgow and back in the summer of 1928 — whilst to the *Puma*, under her later name of *Lairdsford*, belongs the dubious honour of being the only one of the combine's vessels in which I was ever seasick.

LAIRD LINE PASSENGER SHIPS 1919

The more important passenger ships owned by the Laird Line (Alexander Laird and Company) in 1919 were:

Olive	(1893)	1114 grt	260' x 33'		*Rowan*	(1909)	1493 grt	281' x 38'
Lily	(1896)	635 grt	191' x 29'		*Maple*	(1914)	1294 grt	261' x 36'
Rose	(1902)	1098 grt	256' x 36'					

There were also three older vessels — *Briar*, *Broom* and *Thistle* — but these did not survive for long after 1919 and need not concern us here, except to note that the *Broom* was transferred to the Belfast Steamship Company to work solely as a cargo/livestock carrier.

It is now time to look at each of the Burns Laird passenger services which operated between the two world wars.

GLASGOW-BELFAST

The former Burns service between Glasgow and Belfast operated on each week night throughout the year. Unlike the services from Glasgow to Dublin and to Derry, no calls were made at Greenock, from which port a separate cargo-only service to and from Belfast was maintained. Inwards to Glasgow, however, the Belfast ships normally called at Merklands Wharf, a short distance down river from the Broomielaw (the Scottish terminus of the route). At Merklands there were extensive cattle lairages which, at one time, had been the reception centre, not only for Irish livestock, but also for animals from the United States and Canada, before foot and mouth disease regulations put a stop to the transatlantic cattle trade.

Discharging cattle (and to a lesser extent sheep and pigs) could detain an incoming steamer for over an hour and it was common for passengers in a hurry to disembark at Merklands and make their way to the city centre by tram or taxi. The Broomielaw itself was within reasonable walking distance of three of the four Glasgow railway termini (the odd one out was Buchanan Street) but it was not served by any direct tram or bus route. Access facilities for Burns Laird passengers at Donegall Quay, Belfast, were the same as those available (or perhaps one should say unavailable) for travellers to Heysham or Liverpool — one walked or took a taxi.

Until 1930, the ships which normally worked the Glasgow-Belfast service were the *Partridge* and the *Woodcock* but, in that year, those elderly and old-fashioned vessels were replaced by the erstwhile B and I *Lady Limerick* (renamed

Lairdscastle) and *Lady Louth* (renamed *Lairdsburn*). When these ships started their Burns Laird careers, the *Woodcock* was sold to the Aberdeen Steam Navigation Company, who named her *Lochnagar* but the *Partridge*, now the *Lairdsloch*, remained with Burns and Laird until 1936, when she was scrapped. In that year the *Lairdsburn* and *Lairdscastle* were replaced on the 'Direct Route' by two new Coast Lines standard motor ships, *Royal Scotsman* and *Royal Ulsterman*.

The new vessels, each of 3244 grt, on dimensions of 328'x 48', were slightly smaller single-funnelled versions of the 'Ulster' ships of 1929-1930. The internal arrangements for the 'Royals' were generally similar to those of the BSS Co's motor ships, but the smoke room/bar accommodation was smaller, making space available for some first class single-berth cabins on the boat deck. Another difference was that the *Royal Scotsman* and *Royal Ulsterman* had no first class sleeping accommodation below the mid-ship superstructure, whereas the 'Ulsters' had some 'tween deck cabins. In the Glasgow ships, cattle, rather than saloon travellers, occupied the relevant area, except during the height of the holiday season when two-legged third class travellers, rather than four-legged bovine and ovine ones, were given uncomfortable and draughty accommodation immediately below the sleeping berths of their more opulent fellow travellers. There was one very minor point of difference between the *Royal Scotsman* and the *Royal Ulsterman*, which probably went unnoticed by the

World Ship Society

The *Royal Scotsman*, 3244 grt, 328'x 48', built by Harland and Wolff in 1936 for the Belfast-Glasgow service of the Burns and Laird Lines. The vessel remained on this duty, apart from the war years, during her entire life with the company.

great majority of those who travelled in these ships. The former vessel carried a thistle at the top of the foremast, whilst the latter sported a shamrock at the main.

When the new vessels came on to the Belfast service, the *Lairdscastle* and *Lairdsburn* were moved to the Glasgow-Dublin route, though they returned to the Belfast service during the Second World War. It was while so engaged that the *Lairdscastle* was lost following a collision. The *Lairdsburn* survived the war and lasted until 1954, by which time she was thirty-one years old. For most of her final eight years she again ran to and from Dublin, her original home port. However, during the years up to 1953, she regularly appeared in Belfast as relief to each of the 'Royals' when they underwent their annual surveys. I once saw the *Lairdsburn* in Derry but she does not appear to have been a regular visitor to that city.

The *Royal Scotsman* and the *Royal Ulsterman* were built for the Glasgow-Belfast route and, apart from absence on war service, remained on it until they were withdrawn in the late 1960s. So far as I know the only peace time diversion of either of them was in 1937, and probably in 1939, when one of them (in 1937 the *Royal Scotsman*), ran as an extra from Glasgow to Dublin to cater for rugby enthusiasts travelling to an international match. What might be described as semi diversions, however, were regular occurrences during the July holidays of each year when additional Belfast sailings were operated, with the Scottish termini being Greenock and/or Ardrossan.

I had two experiences of passages in the Burns Laird motor ships, other than on their normal schedules. The first of these was the Glasgow-Dublin sailing for the international rugby match in 1937. This was particularly interesting to me, in that it was my first Irish Sea crossing in a Coast Lines standard vessel. When the *Royal Scotsman* arrived in Dublin on that occasion, a member of the crew had to demonstrate the working of the electric winches to the dockers, these items of equipment being then a novelty in Burns Laird ships. My second unusual experience began as a normal embarkation on the *Royal Scotsman* at the Broomielaw on a December evening in 1937, the prelude to an overnight passage to Belfast, but ended with a daylight trip in the *Royal Ulsterman* from Greenock to the Irish port. Dense fog had prevented the latter ship, incoming from Belfast, from travelling further up the Clyde than Greenock, and had also immobilised her sister vessel at the Broomielaw. The *Royal Scotsman*'s passengers, your author among them, were taken by train to Greenock from where, in clear weather, we had an uneventful journey to Belfast. This was the only day passage I made in either of the Burns Laird 'Royals'.

The *Royal Scotsman* and the *Royal Ulsterman* both survived the war, during which they served as troop carriers and infantry landing ships — Iceland, North Africa and Madagascar being but a few of the areas visited by one or other of them.

My last crossing in one of these well-remembered ships was in the *Royal Scotsman* in the early summer of 1967, by which time she had begun to show signs of her age and her hard war service, in the form of engine noise, vibration and numerous squeaks and rattles. However, my very last Belfast-Glasgow journey did not take place until the summer of 1969, in the *Scottish Coast*, my final passage in a Coast Lines 'standard' vessel.

BELFAST-ARDROSSAN

The route from Belfast to Ardrossan was the only one on which Coast Lines operated an express 'short sea' service and even then in summer only. However, throughout the inter-war years up to 1936 the elderly *Magpie* and *Vulture* (from 1929, under their new names of *Lairdsgrove* and *Lairdsrock*), made their measured progress across the seventy nautical miles between Ardrossan and Belfast every night, Monday to Friday, in each direction. Departure from Belfast was at 2145 and arrival in Scotland around 0445. In the reverse direction, the schedules were at somewhat later hours but with much the same overall time. Seventy miles qualified for the title 'short sea', but seven hours scarcely did. It may be wondered why, in the late 1920s and early 1930s and particularly after the introduction of the *Princess Margaret* to the rival Stranraer route, the Ardrossan service, with its slow and antiquated vessels, attracted any significant amount of passenger traffic at other than peak holiday periods. The fact that the old ships continued to be reasonably well patronised until their withdrawal in 1936 was mainly due to two features:

(a)   The service gave a later departure from Belfast than those provided by either the Stranraer or the Glasgow direct route.

(b)   Passengers could arrive very early in the morning in Glasgow, by a direct train from the pier at Ardrossan, a very useful service for those travelling onwards to Scottish provincial destinations. The Stranraer alternative was to arrive in Glasgow at midnight and spend the night at a hotel.

The Ardrossan route was particularly useful to passengers to and from Dublin and places in the south of Ireland, if one did not wish to travel by the long sea route from the Irish capital to Glasgow, or if there was no sailing on that route on a particular night. The latest train from Dublin which gave a connection to the Stranraer, or the Belfast-Glasgow direct services, left at 1515, whereas the 1840 provided a fairly tight, but usually reliable, connection into the Ardrossan steamer. As was the case with passengers by this train travelling onwards by the Belfast-Heysham vessel, the travelling ticket collector checked if there were any passengers for Ardrossan and, if necessary, wired forward from Portadown (the last stop before Belfast) for the ship to be held back for a reasonable time. No doubt on such occasions the *Magpie* or the *Vulture* would exert herself somewhat beyond her customary eleven knots.

As a concrete example of the time saving afforded by the Ardrossan route, I cite the through Edinburgh-Dublin journey. One could leave Edinburgh around 1900, arrive in Dublin at 1100, do virtually a full day's work there and be back in Edinburgh at about 0800 the next morning. In the reverse direction there was a comparable advantage over the competing services. Despite the Ardrossan route's advantages, however, as soon as the *Royal Ulsterman* and *Royal Scotsman* took up service on the direct route, the Ardrossan night passenger ships were withdrawn, although cargo and livestock continued to be carried in two of three new motor ships built by Harland and Wolff — *Lairdsbank*, *Lairdscrest* and *Lairdswood*. (The third of these vessels was appointed to the Derry-Heysham service.)

After 1936 the *Lairdsgrove* was retained by Burns and Laird as a reserve ship, but the *Lairdsrock* went to David MacBrayne, and as *Lochgarry* ran on the Glasgow–West Highland–Stornaway route until she was taken over by the Government for war service. She sank off the north coast of Ireland after being torpedoed on passage between Iceland and the UK in 1942. *Lairdsrock*'s final owners, the old established firm of David MacBrayne, had been reconstituted in 1928 as David MacBrayne (1928) Ltd, under the joint ownership of Coast Lines and the London Midland and Scottish Railway Company.

For some years before 1914, G and J Burns had operated a summer only express 'daylight' service between Ardrossan and Belfast, using the turbine vessel *Viper*, 1713 grt, 315'x 39'6", built in 1906. (*Vulture* and *Viper* are surely two of the most infelicitous names ever carried by Irish Sea vessels.) The Ardrossan day service was not restored until several years after the end of the First World War. Various ships then worked it including, for at least one season, the *Moorfowl*. However, neither this relatively new vessel, nor any other of the company's ships, were suitable for the task, being too slow and having passenger accommodation designed for night rather than day crossings. The lack of a suitable vessel was not made good until 1931, in which year the triple-screw direct-drive turbine steamer *Riviera* was acquired from the Southern Railway. This ship, renamed *Lairdsisle* by her new owners, had been put into service by the erstwhile South Eastern and Chatham Railway's Managing Committee on its English Channel routes in 1911.

The *Riviera* (*Lairdsisle*), built in 1911, was of 1783 grt, on main dimensions of 316'x 41'1". She was a typical early twentieth century railway vessel with two funnels, counter stern and open passenger decks. Under Burns Laird ownership she was an oil burner. The *Lairdsisle* maintained the Ardrossan-Belfast daylight service each summer until the end of August 1939 and again, after the war, until 1953, when she was replaced by the new but slower *Irish Coast*. In the later 1950s this latter vessel was succeeded at Ardrossan by her sister *Scottish Coast*.

The *Lairdsisle*'s speed of twenty-one knots was ample for the passage time of about four hours which, on the journey to Belfast, included the time taken in turning and proceeding astern for some distance to her berth at Donegall Quay and, in both directions, reduced speed on the long approach to Belfast. So far as I remember, the departure time from Ardrossan was about 0945, after the arrival

IOMSP Co

The triple screw turbine vessel *Viper*, 1713 grt, 315′x 39′6″, built by Dennys in 1906 for the Ardrossan-Belfast daylight service of G and J Burns. In 1920 the ship was bought by the Isle of Man Steam Packet Company and renamed *Snaefell*. The picture shows her as an Isle of Man vessel.

of the connecting boat train from Glasgow, whilst in the return direction the ship sailed at 1600. In the inter-war years a train leaving Dublin at 1200 gave an excellent service for passengers from and via that city to passengers for Glasgow, Edinburgh and central and southern Scottish destinations, without any night travel. By leaving Edinburgh on an early morning train one could, thanks to the *Lairdsisle*, be in Dublin at 1730. After the war, the connection ex Dublin was not quite so good, the train leaving at 1100 rather than 1200. In the opposite direction, there was no appreciable change from the pre-war times.

I made only one crossing in the *Lairdsisle,* in the summer of 1937, travelling from Dublin by the aforementioned 1200 train, but I can still remember the main impression the ship made on me — one of almost complete silence. I was accustomed to the whine of turbine gearing from the night crossings I had made between Dun Laoghaire and Holyhead in a berth in the starboard main deck alleyway of one of the mail steamers, right against the engine room casing. Whilst the direct-drive arrangement was less economical in operation than a geared-turbine installation, there was no doubt as to which system provided the pleasanter travelling.

An all the year round daylight service between Ardrossan and Belfast was introduced by Burns and Laird in 1968, using the new ro-ro vessel *Lion* (an

W Grogan

Burns and Laird's *Lairdsisle*, 1783 grt, 316' x 41'1", built by Dennys in 1911 for the South Eastern and Chatham Railways' Managing Committee. She was acquired, as the *Riviera*, by Burns and Laird in 1931 for the summer only Belfast-Ardrossan daylight service. She was withdrawn in 1953.

interesting reversion to the old naming system). The *Lion*, whose vital statistics were 3333 grt, 363'5"x 58', ran to approximately the same timings as those of the *Viper* and the *Lairdsisle* and, having both bow and stern loading arrangements, appeared to be an ideal vessel with which to give new life to the ailing Burns Laird services between the North of Ireland and Scotland. However, it was not to be. The superior attraction of the thirty-six mile 2¼ hour passage from Larne, as opposed to the seventy mile, four hour trip from Belfast, soon made itself felt (particularly for traffic to and from England) and, under her new ownership of P and O, the *Lion* was, in 1971, transferred to one of that company's English Channel services, so far as I remember the one between Portsmouth and Le Havre.

Though I often saw the *Lion* at Donegall Quay I have only the vaguest recollection of her internal arrangements. Externally, she was almost flush decked, with little in the way of superstructure and with twin funnels aft. I travelled once in the ship, from Ardrossan to Belfast. The passage came at the end of a journey from Shetland, of which the first night had been virtually sleepless in the heavily rolling *Saint Ninian* between Lerwick and Kirkwall. The second, after a very lively crossing of the Pentland Firth in the *Saint Ola* and a

Laurence Liddle

The motor ship *Saint Ola*, 750 grt, 178'2"x 33'2", built by Hall Russell and Co, Aberdeen, in 1951 for the North of Scotland, Orkney and Shetland, Shipping Co. *Saint Ola*'s entire life with the company was spent on the hard weather all year round Pentland Firth service, between Stromness (Orkney) and Scrabaster (Thurso), apart from some minor relief work on the North Isles of Shetland route.

six hour train journey from Thurso to Inverness, was also sleepless (even though I was in a 'sleeper' from Inverness to Glasgow), so I was in no condition to appreciate whatever attractions the *Lion* may have had to offer. This must have been the only daylight Irish Sea crossing I ever made, on which I slept for the entire journey.

OTHER BURNS LAIRD SERVICES

Apart from the services to and from Belfast, there were, during part of our period, five other passenger routes served by Burns and Laird. Four of these routes may be considered together since there was a fair amount of interchange of ships between them and the nature of the traffic on each was similar, being characterised by relatively small numbers of passengers during nine and a half months of each year, but with many people travelling between mid June and the end of August. During the weeks of the Scottish holiday fairs all accommodation in every available ship would be occupied. The practice of replacing livestock pens in the 'tween decks by temporary seats, enabled the older vessels in particular to carry many times their usual complements. For example, the 1141 gross ton *Olive / Lairdsbank* was at one time certified for one hundred saloon and

The late Gordon Donaldson's collection

Alexander Laird and Company's *Olive*, 1141 grt, 260'x 43', built in 1893. She was subsequently the *Lairdsbank* and, after her sale to the North of Scotland Co in 1930, the *Saint Catherine*. Alterations made by her new owners reduced her grt to 1047.

one thousand third class passengers. The temporary 'tween deck accommodation was only for passengers travelling steerage, but saloon sleeping facilities could be augmented by making up beds on the settees in the dining saloons and other public rooms (if any). At peak periods the number of services could be increased, to a limited extent, by using Greenock and Ardrossan as terminals, rather than Glasgow and by running some ships as passenger vessels only, thus permitting shorter turn around times. Such operating procedures were, of course, only possible during the height of the holiday season when commercial and industrial activity was much reduced.

Complementing the intensive summer passenger traffic, the cattle trade, always substantial, rose to a peak in October and November. Again, every ship would be in service but with 'tween decks full of four, rather than two, legged passengers and, again, special sailings operated. Particularly during the earlier post Second World War period, there was a considerable amount of 'common user' operation of Burns Laird and British and Irish cargo/livestock ships during the autumn peak period, for cattle traffic. If the B and I *Kilkenny* was well acquainted with Merklands Wharf, neither did the *Lairdsben* have to be taught the way to Birkenhead.

Apropos of the contrast between animal and human occupants of the 'tween decks, I once overheard a question addressed by a foreman docker/drover at

110

Merklands to one of his subordinates, which seemed to indicate a certain confusion as to which species of third class passenger was being carried. The underling had been engaged in the disembarkation of a number of elderly bulls from the *Lairdshill* just arrived from Dublin. As the last of these lumbered along the gangway, the foreman shouted across to his mate, "Hey Hector, is that all the gentlemen?" Seriously though, the loading and unloading of cattle was a noisy and often brutal business, calculated to turn the thoughts of anyone, with a vestige of feeling for animals, in the direction of vegetarianism. I did once hear a docker, assisting in the embarkation of a consignment of lambs onto an LMS vessel in Dublin, adjuring a colleague to "go easy with the lambs", but usually the process was a mixture of shouts, heavy blows with stout sticks and prods with the metal tipped ends of the latter. Where two or three frightened beasts had, as not uncommonly happened, jammed themselves together in the narrow gangway they could be beaten across their faces to get them to back out.

But enough of this less attractive side of cross channel shipping operations.

The four Burns Laird services, just referred to, were those between Glasgow and Dublin, Glasgow and Derry and to and from Heysham and the same two Irish ports. Of these, the two which were based on Glasgow continued to transport passengers, general cargo and livestock until the late 1960s, though

P & O

Burns and Laird's *Lairdsburn*, ex *Lady Louth*, 1870 grt, 277'x 38', which was built in 1923 for the British and Irish Steam Packet Company's Dublin-Liverpool passenger/livestock/general cargo service. The picture shows the vessel disembarking cattle at Merklands Wharf, Glasgow. Note the large cowl ventilators for supplying air to the cattle pens.

passengers were not carried between Dublin and Glasgow during the war years. The frequency of sailings on these Dublin and Derry routes varied but, in the 1930s, and apart from seasonal extras for passengers or stock, the pattern was for there to be from four to six nightly sailings per week in each direction, according to the time of year and the general state of trade. For many years the basic service between Glasgow and Dublin provided for ships to leave Glasgow (Anderston Quay, adjacent to the Broomielaw) on Monday, Wednesday, Friday and Saturday afternoons, or evenings, and to sail from North Wall, Dublin on Mondays, Wednesdays, Thursdays and Saturdays at 1700 or 1800. The two absolutely fixed sailing days were Wednesday ex-Glasgow, and Thursday ex-Dublin, since the cattle market in the latter city was held on Thursdays. Passage times varied slightly, according to what ships were on the route, but about fourteen hours from Dublin to arriving at, or passing, Greenock and a further two hours to Merklands, was usual. From Merklands to Anderston Quay, allowing for the ship having to turn before coming alongside the terminal berth, occupied a further half hour or so. Comparable times, but with no delays at Merklands, obtained in the reverse direction.

The importance of the Dublin cattle market as a feeder of the cross channel livestock trade, was reflected in the normal Thursday line up of ships along the North Wall quay. Nearest to the city centre would be the *Assaroe* for Silloth, followed immediately, to the east of the entrance to the Custom House docks, by two B and I cargo vessels, followed by that company's Liverpool passenger ship. Further east again, past the entrance to the Royal Canal dock, would be two vessels on the Holyhead cargo service. Immediately beyond this was the Burns Laird berth, with usually (after 1927) just one ship alongside but occasionally, at the height of the autumn cattle season, there might be a second. At such times too, there could be another B and I ship standing by at Sir John Rogerson's Quay, just across the river from North Wall.

The pattern of Glasgow-Derry sailings was generally similar to that which obtained on the Dublin route, though the normal timetable from Derry provided for a Friday, and not a Thursday, sailing. After about 1933, calls at Greenock were made more often by the Derry, than by the Dublin, steamers.

Operation of the two basic four nights per week services needed a minimum of four ships. At a pinch, six nights per week could be managed by five vessels but, since this entailed using only two on the Derry route, turn around time in Glasgow would be limited if a large number of cattle had to be disembarked. Of the two routes, it was the Derry one which saw the greater seasonal fluctuations in passenger traffic. During the July holidays, it was not uncommon for the regular service ex-Glasgow to be run in duplicate, apart altogether from any special sailings. I remember a summer evening passage down the Clyde in the *Lairdsmoor* bound for Dublin, closely followed by both the *Lairdsglen* and the *Lairdsrose* for Derry.

Neither of the passenger services to and from Heysham lasted throughout the inter-war years. The Dublin route, directly competitive with the B and I's cargo/livestock service to Preston, was abandoned entirely in 1927. Its Derry

P & O

The Burns and Laird's *Lairdsrose*, 1098 grt, launched in 1902 as the *Rose* for Alexander Laird and Company, was a long time regular on the Glasgow-Derry route. She survived two World Wars and was not withdrawn until 1951, 49 years old – a venerable lady indeed. The photograph dates from 1936 or later.

counterpart lost its passenger service in 1933, although freight and livestock continued to be handled for a further thirty-five years.

Mention of the Dublin to Preston service reminds me that, when this route was acquired by the British and Irish from the erstwhile Dublin and Lancashire Shipping Company in 1923, the former concern took over the steamship *Brussels*, 1090 grt, 285'3"x 34', built in 1901. This vessel, which was formerly owned by the Great Eastern Railway Company, had achieved a considerable amount of publicity during the 1914-18 war, on account of her master, Captain Fryatt, having been captured and shot by German forces. So far as I know, this former Harwich-based vessel was the only two funnelled ship owned by the B and I Line, before it took over the ex BSS Co trio in 1929 and supplied them each with an extra funnel. Her new owners renamed the *Brussels* by the simple expedient of adding the word *Lady* to her original title.

DUBLIN AND DERRY SHIPS

The ships which worked these four Burns Laird services during the 1920s and 1930s, are listed below, together with some relevant details. Figures for tonnage, main dimensions and dates of building have already been noted.

Lairdscastle (ex *Lady Limerick*) and *Lairdsburn* (ex *Lady Louth*)

Reference to these vessels in both their B and I and Burns Laird incarnations has already been made.

P & O

The Burns and Laird steamer *Lairdsglen*, 1294 grt, formerly Alexander Laird and Company's *Maple*, built in 1914. During the inter-war years this was the most versatile of all the Burns and Laird smaller passenger vessels, likely to be found on any of the secondary routes at any time. During the Second World War she spent a short time on charter work between Fishguard and Rosslare. She was withdrawn for scrapping in 1951.

Lairdsbank (ex *Olive*)

This ship ran mostly on the Derry services, to and from both Glasgow and Heysham. In 1930 she was sold to the North of Scotland, Orkney and Shetland Steam Navigation Company, for whom as *Saint Catherine*, she worked until 1937, when she was withdrawn and scrapped. In her days as a 'North Company' ship she ran mostly on the Leith-Aberdeen-Lerwick 'direct' route.

Lairdsford (ex *Puma* ex *Duke of Rothesay*)

The *Lairdsford* ran latterly on both the Dublin and the Derry routes but, towards the end of her days, as a relief vessel rather than as a regular. She lasted until the mid 1930s.

Lairdsforest (ex *Tiger*, ex *Duke of Montrose*)

This ship ran mostly on the Dublin-Glasgow service for which she had been built. In 1929/30 she went to the B and I as *Lady Louth*, but for freight and livestock duties only. She was scrapped in 1934.

Lairdsglen (ex *Maple*)

The *Lairdsglen* was the most versatile of all the secondary ships. She was liable to turn up in either Dublin or Derry at any time and she worked the last passenger sailing from Heysham to Derry. At the Christmas and New Year period of 1943/44 she ran on charter, for a short while, between Rosslare and Fishguard, as a third class only vessel. I do not know if this restriction was because the FRRH Co considered that her first class facilities were of only third class standard. This ship survived the Second World War (as she had the First) but was disposed of, presumably for scrapping, in 1951.

Lairdsgrove (ex Magpie)

After the closure of the Ardrossan-Belfast night passenger service, this ship was available for extra passenger or livestock services as required. She lasted until 1948.

Lairdshill (ex Lady Longford, ex Ardmore)

This ship was regularly on the Dublin service until 1936, when she went back to the British and Irish and again became Lady Longford. However, in the following year she returned to Burns and Laird for a second spell as Lairdshill, as a consequence of the loss of the Lairdsmoor (see below). She remained on the Dublin route, apart from wartime diversions, until she was scrapped in 1957. These diversions included operating to and from Belfast after the loss of the Lairdscastle. The return of this ship to Burns Laird in 1937 meant that, at the height of the summer seasons of that year and the two following ones, the Glasgow-Dublin route was operating to a higher standard than ever before — a nightly service maintained by three relatively new oil-burning vessels.

Early in 1933 the Lairdshill was storm and snow bound for about twenty-four hours in Dublin Bay. The incident attracted some notice in the press, as the ship had the Scottish international rugby team on board.

Finally, as regards the Lairdshill, at some time during the Second World War she had her masts and funnel shortened, an operation which, whatever the reason for it, did nothing to improve her appearance. It was perhaps fitting that this ship, which was so closely associated with the port of Dublin during her long career under two nominal owners, should have been scrapped there. So far as I know, it was the only Coast Lines or railway vessel of the inter-war years to have been broken up there.

Lairdsloch (ex Partridge)

As a general reserve ship between 1930 and 1936, this vessel was often on the Dublin route during the summers of those years, when a six night per week service was in operation. My parents, my two brothers and I travelled to and from Glasgow in the Lairdsloch en route to and from a holiday in Edinburgh in 1932. Used as we were to the LMS Holyhead mail steamers, we were not impressed by what this Burns Laird antique had to offer in the way of accommodation. Indeed we always remembered the ship as a noisy and dirty old stinker.

Lairdsmoor (ex Moorfowl, ex Killarney)

During the 1930s, this ship (of which I have only pleasant memories, despite my comments on page six) was, towards the end of her days, regularly on the Dublin-Glasgow service, until her loss from stranding south of Corsewall Point during a fog, early in 1937. There was little loss of human life but her master did not survive. The *Lairdsmoor* and the *Lairdshill* were the most modern ships to run between Dublin and Glasgow before 1936-7. Like the *Lairdshill*, the *Lairdsmoor* was an oil burner, having been converted in 1926.

Lairdsrose (ex *Rose*)

This ex-Laird Line vessel was almost an institution on the Glasgow-Derry service. I do not remember ever having seen her in Dublin. Her last listing in Lloyds' Register was in the 1949/50 edition.

Lairdsvale (ex *Pointer*)

This was another ship which turned up in Derry more often than in Dublin, though I remember seeing her in Dublin during the Christmas holiday period of 1932. Like the *Lairdsford*, this vessel was disposed of during the later 1930s.

GLASGOW — WEST OF IRELAND

The final Burns Laird (formerly Laird) Line passenger service to be noted is the very minor operation between Glasgow and Sligo, Ballina and Westport. The only ship which I ever saw on this route was the *Lily/Lairdspool*. This little ship had no passenger certificate after 1934 but my recollection (admittedly of matters over sixty years ago) is that some passengers were carried on the west of Ireland service until 1936. Since, by 1934, the *Lairdspool* was the last remaining small passenger vessel of the Burns Laird Company, she may have had a twelve-passenger certificate during her last two years with that firm. She ended her days with David Macbrayne as *Lochgorm*. This relatively insignificant member of the then Laird fleet, was the first ship of the Coast Lines combine which I can definitely remember seeing. During some time spent with my parents in the west of Ireland in 1924, my father having professional commitments there, we stayed for about a month in Rosses Point at the entrance to Sligo Harbour. During that time the regular comings and goings of the *Lily* were a source of considerable interest to your nine year old author.

Until the mid-1930s, some west of Ireland services terminated in Sligo, whilst others served Ballina and Westport also. (At one time, an ex-Clyde puffer, the *Tartar*, had provided a freight connection from Ballina to Belmullet.) Irrespective of the number of ports served, however, there was rarely more than one departure per week from Glasgow. Whilst there may have been a few holiday makers who used the service during the summer months, it is likely that, at any rate after the First World War, the bulk of such passenger traffic as there was by the service, was provided by the considerable number of migratory labourers travelling to and from their work on Scottish farms.

In 1936 Burns and Laird took over the Sligo Steam Navigation Company's freight and livestock service between Sligo and Liverpool. (The SSN Co was already a Coast Lines subsidiary.) With the acquisition of this service, Burns and Laird became the owners of the twinscrew steamship *Sligo*, 891 grt, 221'x 35',

(Continued on page 119)

Barry Carse

The B and I SP Co's motor ship *Munster*, 4142 grt, built by Harland and Wolff in 1948. The picture was very probably taken in 1967 or early in 1968, and shows the ship at the traditional B and I passenger berth at North Wall Quay, Dublin. A photo of this ship under her later name of *Orpheus* appears on page 94.

Brian Boyle

Scottish Coast of 1957, 3817 grt, at Donegall Quay, Belfast in the late 1960s, when operating on Burns and Lairds' Belfast-Glasgow overnight service. The vessel ahead of her is British Rail's *Duke of Argyll*, 4797 grt, built by Harland and Wolff in 1956 for the Heysham-Belfast service.

Barry Carse

Douglas harbour, with *Manxman*, the last of the standard ships, built in 1955, in the foreground. A second standard vessel is alongside the outer side of the far pier. The third ship is *Lady of Mann*, built in 1930 and the last survivor of the pre-war ships.

Barry Carse

The turbine steamer *Manx Maid*, 2724 grt, built for the IOMSP Co, in 1962, by Cammell Laird. *Manx Maid* was the pioneer of the four ro-ros owned by the company during its independent existence. The picture shows the ship at North Wall, Dublin, in 1974, the year in which the last of the quartet, MS *Lady of Mann* entered service.

P & O

The steamship *Sligo*, 891 grt, 221'x 35', built in 1930 for the Sligo Steam Navigation Company's freight and livestock service between Sligo and Liverpool. In 1936 the Sligo company was merged with Burns and Laird, and the *Sligo* became the *Lairdsdale*, under which name she is pictured here. Unusually for a vessel of her type the *Sligo* was a twin screw ship.

built in 1930. The separate Glasgow and Liverpool services were amalgamated into a single triangular one, Sligo-Glasgow-Liverpool-Sligo, operated by the *Sligo*, renamed *Lairdsdale*. No passengers were carried and Ballina and Westport lost their direct communication with Glasgow. This revised service ran approximately weekly until the outbreak of war, after which it became irregular and was never fully reinstated, although there were some sailings, at any rate from Liverpool, until the mid 1950s. The *Lairdsdale*, however, remained as an active unit of the Burns Laird fleet for a number of years. By the end of her life, the erstwhile *Sligo* had changed her identity, to become the *Ulster Drover* of the Belfast Steamship Company, an appropriate, if scarcely elegant, name.

POST-WAR SERVICES

For a short time after the end of the Second World War, the situation, as regards the Dublin and the Derry passenger services, was more or less comparable to what it had been in the 1930s. The *Lairdsburn* and *Lairdshill* usually operated to and from Dublin, whilst the new MS *Lairdsloch*, 1736 grt, 275'x 41'2", built in 1944, and the veteran *Lairdsrose* maintained the Derry service. The evergreen *Lairdsglen* and (until 1948) the *Lairdsgrove* provided relief and extra summer services.

It was not long, however, before the Dublin and the Derry services began to feel the competition from the airlines and the increasing attraction and

P & O

The Burns and Laird steamship *Lairdscraig*, 1599 grt, 282'x 38', which was built in 1936 as the *Rathlin* for the Clyde Shipping Company. She was bought by Burns and Laird in 1953 but in 1956 was transferred to the City of Cork Steam Packet Co (B and I Line), where she became the *Glengariff*. This vessel served as a convoy rescue ship during the Second World War.

availability of continental holidays, whilst improved pay and working conditions for ships' crews and shore staff, ate into receipts. One by one the older ships were disposed of and the frequency of services reduced until, by 1954, there remained just the *Lairdshill* to serve Dublin and the *Lairdsloch* for the Derry route. Passenger sailings on each service were stabilised at two per week, in each direction, for most of the year, with the extra summer traffic being provided for by running each ship as a passenger-only vessel, thus enabling thrice weekly services to be operated. The acquisition of three new cargo/cattle vessels — *Lairdsmoor*, 1949; *Lairdsben*, 1951 and *Lairdsglen*, 1956 — ensured that there was no deterioration in freight and livestock facilities. Some additional passenger accommodation had become available in 1953 with the acquisition of the Clyde Shipping Company's *Rathlin*, 1599 grt, 282'x 38'. This single-screw steamship, which was renamed *Lairdscraig*, was of the same general type as the *Moorfowl / Lairdsmoor* and *Maple / Lairdsglen*. She had been built in 1936 for her original owners' Glasgow-London service and, during the war, had served as a convoy rescue ship. However the *Lairdscraig* did not remain long with Burns and Laird. In 1956 she was transferred to the City of Cork section of the B and I Line and, under yet another name – *Glengariff* – took up station on the Cork to Liverpool route.

The standards of accommodation provided on the Dublin-Glasgow service were greatly improved in 1957, when the *Scottish Coast* succeeded the thirty-six year old *Lairdshill*. The vessel was soon replaced by her sister *Irish Coast*. However, this did not entail any reduction in standards and so, for the last twelve years of its operation, the Dublin-Glasgow route was for the first time offering standards, amenities and facilities fully equal to (if not indeed better than) those obtaining on all the other major routes of Coast Lines.

Although the Dublin service had to wait until 1957 before being provided with an up to date ship, the major improvement for Derry passengers came as early as 1945, when the *Lairdsloch*, which in her very early days had operated as a cargo vessel, entered passenger service. This motor ship was basically of the same design as the *Lairdscraig*, though with her large, but low, semi-streamlined funnel and broad beam, she somewhat resembled a miniature 'standard' vessel at first sight.

I was never aboard the *Lairdsloch* and indeed one of my great regrets is that, during the years when I had the opportunity, I never travelled by the Derry-Glasgow route. She was the last passenger vessel to operate regularly out of Derry and, from what I could determine from my many scrutinies of her when she was in her Irish berth, she had the usual saloon sleeping accommodation in the major part of her full beam midship structure, together with two rather small public rooms — dining saloon and bar / general room — one on either side of the ship at the forward end. So far as I could ascertain, her steerage accommodation was not all that much better than that which had been provided in earlier ships.

W Grogan

The Coast Lines' standard vessel *Irish Coast*, 3813 grt, 339'8"x 51'7", built by Harland and Wolff in 1953. The ship is shown here passing Dumbarton Rock on the north bank of the river Clyde, between Greenock and Glasgow. It is likely that on this occasion she was working on Burns and Laird's Dublin-Glasgow service.

Right to the end, the time honoured custom of packing the steerage passengers into the 'tween deck cattle area at the height of the summer season prevailed with both *Lairdsloch* and *Irish Coast*.

The *Lairdsloch* was withdrawn and sold to an Israeli firm in 1969, in which year the Derry passenger route was abandoned. The Dublin service came to an end at about the same time, when the *Irish Coast* was 'sold foreign' in 1968. She went to the Greek Epirotiki Lines.

CITY OF CORK STEAM PACKET COMPANY

We must now take a look at the City of Cork Steam Packet Company, to and from which a succession of ships came and went in the early inter-war years.

The *Killarney*, delivered in 1919, was very soon transferred to G and J Burns, who renamed her *Moorfowl*. However, in 1923 the *Lady Killiney*, built in 1918 (as Tedcastle's *Killiney*), came to Cork as the *Ardmore*. Just previously, the City of Cork Company's new *Ardmore*, built in 1921, had been moved to the B and I, where she was renamed *Lady Longford*. However, her twin sister, *Kenmare*, remained a Cork-based ship throughout her long life. In 1927 the City of Cork concern took over the elderly *Classic* (ex *Magic*), of the Belfast Steamship Company, renaming her *Killarney* (her third name).

The final outcome of all this interchanging of vessels was that in the later 1920s the CCSP Co's passenger fleet consisted of:

Killarney	(t s s)	1893	1627 grt	311' x 38'
Kenmare	(s s)	1921	1673 grt	275' x 38'
Ardmore	(s s)	1918	1145 grt	255' x 36'

The passenger routes which operated from 1919 onwards were from Cork to Fishguard and from Cork to Liverpool, though in earlier days both Bristol and London had had passenger services from Cork.

The *Killarney* was long and low, with midship and after superstructures each one deck high, narrow side decks and two funnels. Her twin screws were powered by triple-expansion engines. In 1931 this old ship was transferred yet again, this time to the direct ownership of Coast Lines. After an extensive refit and the provision of some extra passenger accommodation, which included the extension of the dining room into the fore 'tween decks and the raising of the bridge to provide some 'boat deck' cabins, she spent the next eight years operating Coast Lines' summer cruise service from Liverpool and Ardrossan to the west and north coasts of Scotland and to the Western Isles. Occasionally she got as far as Orkney and Inverness.

As part of her reincarnation, the old *Magic* was given a grey hull and yellow funnels and was advertised as SY (steam yacht) *Killarney*! How appropriate the designation 'yacht' was for the veteran Irish Sea plodder, is a matter of opinion. What is indisputable, however, is that Coast Lines seemed to like the word since, in the 1930s, the company was the (possibly) proud possessor of two 'yachts'. The *Killarney*'s companion was the *Lochaline*, another old relic which had been tarted up and painted white and was used as the private pleasure boat of Sir Alfred Reid, the chairman of Coast Lines.

Not only had the *Killarney* had three nominal owners by the 1930s but, in 1934 at any rate, when our family sampled her attractions for a fortnight, her officers came from several sources within the combine. For instance the Master was a Burns Laird man, whilst the Chief Engineer came from the City of Cork company. No doubt it was previous experience with the forty years old machinery of the 'yacht' that recommended the latter for the post. The Third Mate was normally employed by the parent company. The reason why three deck officers were carried, was presumably on account of the considerable amount of boat work that was entailed in bringing passengers to and from the ship when, as was often the case, she was anchored out in a loch. Since there were no cargo operations and since also the vessel was never at sea for more than a few hours out of each twenty-four (except during the first and last nights of the cruise, when she was making the passage between Liverpool and Ardrossan), two mates could surely have coped with all duties other than boat work.

So much for the *Killarney* and her £15 (minimum rate) thirteen day cruises. The next City of Cork ship to be considered is the *Kenmare*. This vessel was almost a mirror image of the *Ardmore/Lady Longford/Lairdshill*. The only immediately apparent difference between them was that whilst the *Kenmare*, in her later days at any rate, carried two boats per side amidships, the sister vessel had three. The *Kenmare* is best remembered as being the regular ship on the Cork-Liverpool service during the 1930s and again from the end of the Second World War until 1957 when, as we have seen, she was withdrawn and replaced by the *Glengariff* (ex *Lairdscraig/Rathlin*). Occasionally in the 1930s, the *Kenmare* worked on the Cork-Fishguard service, for which indeed she had been built, and she ran sporadically between these two ports during the war years. The vessel's regular timetable on the Liverpool route was to leave Cork on a Saturday afternoon/evening and, after a call at Birkenhead to land livestock, arrive at Liverpool landing stage, or Princes Dock, at about 1600 on the Sunday. She left Liverpool again early on Thursday and was back in Cork on Friday morning. This was scarcely an exhausting schedule, but it would have left time to work an extra cattle sailing from Cork, if required. Whether this was ever done, I do not know. From 1936 the *Kenmare*, like other City of Cork ships, was registered under the ownership of the B and I Line, though her port of registry continued to be Cork and, unlike the *Ardmore* (ex *Lady Killiney*), she kept her white, black-topped, funnel colours until the end.

The third Cork passenger vessel, the *Ardmore*, which, however, had lost her passenger certificate by the early 1930s, has already had her career and sad end referred to.

The *Killarney*, the *Kenmare* and the *Ardmore* were all satisfactory and (as

J Clarkson

The *Kenmare*, 1673 grt, 275'x 38', built for the City of Cork Steam Packet Company in 1921. Although this ship was built for the Cork-Fishguard service, from 1931 onwards she spent most of her time running between Cork and Liverpool.

D B McNeill

The motor ship *Innisfallen*, 3071 grt, 321' x 46', built by Harland and Wolff for the Cork-Fishguard route of the City of Cork Steam Packet Company in 1931. This typical Harland and Wolff vessel sank in the Mersey in the autumn of 1940, after striking a mine.

regards the first two) ultimately long serving vessels of their types and periods. However, when one recalls the Cork company's passenger services of the 1930s, the ship that is remembered above all others is the *Innisfallen*. This vessel, the fourth in the series of Coast Lines standard motor ships, came from Harland and Wolff's Belfast yard in 1931. In appearance, she resembled the 'Ulsters' of 1929-30, with two funnels of contemporary motor ship design. With a tonnage of 3071 and dimensions of 321'x 46', she was slightly smaller than the, yet to be built, Burns Laird 'Royals' and a full twenty-five feet shorter than the 'Ulsters', though with a similar beam measurement.

The *Innisfallen* was as great an advance on the *Kenmare* (not to mention the *Killarney*), as the *Ulster Monarch* and consorts had been on the *Patriotic*, *Heroic* and *Graphic*. She attracted an increasing number of travellers to the Cork-Fishguard route, which was henceforth advertised as 'The *Innisfallen* Way'. This service operated ex-Cork at about 1800 on Mondays, Wednesdays and Fridays and was due in Fishguard around 0200 the following morning. On the return passage, the ship left at midnight on Tuesdays, Thursdays and Saturdays and was due in Cork at 0900 next day. There were direct rail connections to and from Swansea, Cardiff and London, at the quayside at Fishguard but the Cork terminal at Penrose Quay, though close to the city centre, had no immediate rail facilities for passengers. It was, however, only a short walk away from the city's main station at Glanmire Road.

The overall time between Cork and London, and other places in Britain, was somewhat less via Rosslare, to and from which a regular boat train served Cork, than by 'direct boat' but, unless time was of the essence, the greater size and comfort of the *Innisfallen*, together with the fact that one avoided the rail/ship transfer at Rosslare, ensured that the new motor vessel never lacked patrons. Not that the Cork-Fishguard crossing, the most exposed of all the Irish cross channel routes, always provided smooth sailing. I well remember a Cork businessman telling me that he had had many a boisterous journey in the *Innisfallen*. However, from my own experience, he could have had just as rough a time in the *Saint Andrew* or one of her consorts, although the discomfort might not have lasted so long.

The *Innisfallen* ran regularly on the Fishguard route from the time of her introduction until the beginning of the Second World War, except for a period in 1935 when she was transferred to the Belfast-Glasgow service, presumably to test the feasibility of operating standard motor ships on that route. I have heard that the *Innisfallen*'s temporary replacement between Cork and Fishguard was the *Lairdsmoor*. If this was the case, and at first sight it seems somewhat unlikely, the reason may have been because this relatively small member of the Burns Laird fleet was faster than either the *Lairdscastle* or *Lairdsburn*, one of which vessels might have been expected to have been used. It is interesting to note that, during her brief service with Burns and Laird, the *Innisfallen* made a round trip between Glasgow and Dublin, duplicating the regular Friday sailing from Glasgow on the occasion of a Scotland versus Ireland rugby match. It is likely, therefore, that this Cork-Fishguard vessel was the first Coast Lines standard ship to visit Dublin.

Like the *Kenmare* and the *Ardmore*, the *Innisfallen* was, from 1936, registered in B and I ownership but, as was the case with the former vessel, she kept her Cork port of registry and her white funnels. In September 1939 the ship was put on the Dublin-Liverpool service, where she continued to run until the late autumn of 1940, when she sank off New Brighton at the mouth of the Mersey, outward bound for Dublin. It was an ironical sinking, in that the vessel had just come unscathed through a heavy air raid. The probable cause of the sinking was a mine dropped by one of the raiding planes. It is a grim commentary on the all-embracing nature of sea warfare that, of the eight ships of the combined British and Irish and City of Cork fleets which remained on the Irish register after the outbreak of war (and thus were neutral vessels), four – *Munster*, *Innisfallen*, *Ardmore* and the 1500 ton cargo/livestock ship *Meath* – were lost, the *Meath* by a mine off Holyhead.

In 1947, the loss of the *Innisfallen* was made good by a namesake, which was slightly larger than her predecessor and sported one funnel only (see page 72). This ship, the third *Innisfallen*, was the first of the five standard Coast Lines vessels to be delivered after the war and the only one, of the total of thirteen, which was not built by Harlands. She came from Dennys of Dumbarton. In the late 1950s and early 1960s it was commonly said that, of the thirteen standard ships, four — the *Royal Scotsman*, *Royal Ulsterman* and the two *Innisfallens*, were 'short wheelbase' models — whilst the other nine — three 'Ulsters', two *Leinsters*, two *Munsters*, the *Irish Coast* and the *Scottish Coast* — were of the 'long wheelbase' type. Finally, as regards the 1947 *Innisfallen*, there is an interesting reverse parallel between her building and that of the LMS Railway's *Duke of York* in 1935. All LMS steamers of the inter-war years, except the *Duke of York*, came from Dennys, whilst that ship was a product of Harland and Wolff. All the Coast Lines standard vessels, except the Denny built *Innisfallen*, came from Harlands.

The Cork-Fishguard service ceased to operate in 1968, and the *Innisfallen*, like most of the other standard ships, was sold in due course to Mediterranean buyers. However, the British and Irish/City of Cork concern (which was acquired by the Irish Government from Coast Lines in 1966) did not abandon Cork for some years. Nevertheless, there was an appreciable gap before yet another *Innisfallen*, which has already been referred to in the British and Irish section, was delivered and inaugurated a new service between Cork and Swansea. As recently as 1994, this 1969 *Innisfallen*, disposed of by the B and I in 1980/81, was operating between Guayaquil (Ecuador) and the Galapagos Islands. The British and Irish did not long continue with the Swansea service. However, the company (now a division of Irish Ferries) is still prominent in the cross channel trade from the south of Ireland, with its twice daily ro-ro service between Rosslare and Pembroke Dock. More recently, there has been a partial restoration of the Cork-Swansea route, tourist and other local interests in those cities having combined to establish a seasonal ro-ro service, using chartered vessels.

W Grogan

The *Glengariff*, ex *Lairdscraig*, ex *Rathlin*. Details of this ship, which succeeded the *Kenmare* on the Cork-Liverpool service, have already been given. Note that the traditional white and black funnel markings of the City of Cork S P Co were retained, even though this was legally a B and I ship.

Finally, what of the Cork-Liverpool passenger route? The *Glengariff* continued her regular weekly crossings until 1968, when yet another ex Burns Laird ship — the cargo/livestock MS *Lairdsbank*, dating from 1936 — was transferred to Cork as the *Glanmire* and saw out the last few remaining years of this long established service.

MINOR COMPANIES

Two small cross channel concerns were absorbed by Coast Lines early this century. Each of these had operated passenger services which, however, were abandoned by the combine. Nevertheless, since two of the three routes which had been served by these formerly independent companies were maintained for cargo and livestock for many years, it is appropriate to mention them briefly. The companies were the Ayr Steamship Company and the Dundalk and Newry Steam Packet Company, which lost their identities within Burns and Laird and the British and Irish respectively. In their independent days the Ayr SS Co had maintained a passenger/cargo/livestock service between Ayr and Belfast whilst the Dundalk and Newry had traded between these two Irish ports and Liverpool, and to a lesser extent, Glasgow. The services retained by Coast Lines were Ayr-Belfast and Liverpool-Dundalk/Newry.

When the British and Irish took over the Dundalk concern in 1927, the only operational passenger carrying vessel acquired was the *Iveagh*, renamed in traditional B and I style, *Lady Iveagh*. This addition to the British and Irish fleet was a single-screw steamship, built in 1872 and certified for seventy saloon and three hundred third class passengers. She was very soon disposed of and replaced by the cargo vessel *Lady Cavan*, formerly the *Wexfordian* of the Wexford Steamship Company. A second passenger ship, the *Bessbrook* of 1877, was also taken over. She was almost immediately sold for scrapping and, so far as I know, never worked for her new owners. To be fair to the memory of the long gone Dundalk and Newry Steam Packet Company, that concern had at one time possessed one ship which was considerably more attractive than either of the two old relics just mentioned. This was the twin-screw *Dundalk* — 863 grt, 236′x 32′2″, built in 1899. Tragically this vessel was lost, after being torpedoed in October 1918, less than four weeks before the end of the war. There were only eleven survivors.

The passenger ships acquired by Coast Lines/Burns Laird from the Ayr Steamship Company were the *Culzean*, 883 grt, 236′x 31′2″, and the *Cairnsmore*, 877 grt, which had virtually identical overall measurements. Each had been built in 1896. These vessels had come to the Ayr concern from the Belfast Steamship Company, under whose ownership they had been the *Logic* and the *Comic*. The *Culzean* and *Cairnsmore* retained these names during their Burns Laird careers but in 1929, when they were transferred to the British and Irish, they became the *Lady Carlow* and *Lady Kerry* respectively. They worked as cargo and livestock carriers under their new house flag until the mid 1930s. I often used to see them

J McRoberts

The *Lady Carlow*, ex *Logic*, ex *Culzean*, 883 grt, 236′x 31′2″. Built in 1896 for the Belfast Steamship Company, this vessel subsequently passed into the hands of the Ayr Steamship Company and became a Burns and Laird ship when the latter concern took over the Ayr Company. In 1929 the *Culzean* was transferred to the B and I Line, for whom she worked as the cargo/livestock ship *Lady Carlow* until the mid 1930s.

in Dublin, engaged in their humdrum task of ferrying bullocks to Birkenhead, and bacon and eggs to Liverpool.

FLEET LISTS

So much for a review of the Irish Sea passenger services of the Coast Lines group of companies and the vessels which operated them during the fifty odd years after the First World War. All that now remains is to list the ships in use in August 1939, and at the end of 1966, the year before the introduction of the group's first Irish Sea ro-ro service.

COAST LINES COMBINE - Irish Sea Passenger Fleet, August 1939

Burns and Laird Lines

Standard Vessels						
Royal Scotsman	1936	3244 grt		Lairdsburn	1923	1870 grt
Royal Ulsterman	1936	3244 grt		Lairdshill	1921	1776 grt
				Lairdsgrove	1898	1247 grt
				Lairdsglen	1914	1294 grt
Non-standard vessels				Lairdsisle	1911	1783 grt
Lairdscastle	1924	1945 grt		Lairdsrose	1902	1098 grt

Belfast Steamship Company

British and Irish/City of Cork Steam Packet Companies.

Standard Vessels				Standard Vessels		
Ulster Monarch	1929	3791 grt		Innisfallen	1931	3071 grt
Ulster Prince	1930	3791 grt		Leinster [1]	1937	4302 grt
Ulster Queen	1930	3791 grt		Munster	1938	4305 grt
Non-standard vessels				Non-standard Vessels [2]		
Nil				Lady Connaught	1912	2284 grt
				Kenmare	1921	1673 grt

Notes:

[1] *Leinster*, though operated as a B and I ship, was registered under the direct ownership of Coast Lines.

[2] *Longford*, formerly *Lady Connaught*, and *Louth*, formerly *Lady Munster*, were, in 1939, still nominally British and Irish ships, but were not in regular service.

COAST LINES COMBINE - *Irish Sea Passenger Fleet, December 1966*

Belfast Steamship Company

Standard Vessels

Ulster Monarch [3]	1929	3851 grt
Ulster Prince [4]	1937	4307 grt

Non-standard Vessels

Nil

Burns and Laird Lines

Standard Vessels

Royal Scotsman	1936	3244 grt
Royal Ulsterman	1936	3244 grt
Scottish Coast [5]	1957	3817 grt

Non-standard vessel

Lairdsloch	1944	1736 grt

British and Irish/City of Cork Steam Packet Companies

Standard Vessels

Innisfallen	1947	3741 grt
Leinster	1948	4115 grt
Munster	1948	4142 grt

Non-standard Vessel

Glengariff	1936	1599 grt

Coast Lines

Standard Vessel

Irish Coast [6]	1953	3813 grt

Notes:
[3] Revised grt after post-war refit
[4] Ex *Leinster*
[5] *Scottish Coast* was registered in the ownership of Burns and Laird Lines but, with her port of registry Liverpool, not Glasgow. She was the regular vessel on Burns Laird's summer service between Ardrossan and Belfast but otherwise was employed as a relief ship for all the Irish Sea passenger companies within the combine.
[6] *Irish Coast* was registered at Liverpool and was directly owned by Coast Lines but was permanently employed on Burns and Laird's Glasgow-Dublin service.

Funnel and hull colours, August 1939

Belfast Steamship Company

Funnels red with black top and a thin blue line immediately below the black. The three 'Ulsters' had grey hulls and white upper-works.

British and Irish Steam Packet Company

Funnels green with black tops. There was a thin white line below the black, a feature which dated from 1937/8. *Leinster* and *Munster* had straw coloured hulls. *Lady Connaught* had a grey hull, a reminder of her BSS Co origins.

Burns and Laird Lines

Funnels as for BSS Co's vessels, hulls black. The 'Royals' had light buff upper-works, other vessels white. The thin blue line on the funnels first appeared on the 'Royals' in 1936, in which year the BSS Co also adopted it.

City of Cork Steam Packet Co (B and I Line)

Although this company had been merged with the British and Irish in 1936, the *Innisfallen* and the *Kenmare* retained their traditional white, black topped funnels although, by 1939, the *Ardmore*, no longer a passenger vessel, had a standard British and Irish funnel. The hulls of all three ships were black with white upper-works.

Wartime funnel and hull colours

During the Second World War, all UK registered ships were painted in an all over grey — hulls, upper-works and funnels. Irish registered vessels had black hulls and funnels and dark straw coloured upper-works. They carried neutrality markings on their sides.

130

Hull and funnel colours 1966

Belfast Steamship Company
    As in 1939 except that hulls were black.

British and Irish SP Co
    Leinster and *Munster* had dark green hulls. Funnel colours were the same as in 1939.

Burns and Laird Lines
    As for Belfast Steamship Co's vessels.

City of Cork Steam Packet Company (B and I Line)
    Funnel and hull colours for *Innisfallen* and *Glengariff* were the same as those for *Innisfallen* and *Kenmare* in 1939. It is perhaps worth noting that, after the British and Irish Company was acquired by the Irish Government, the funnel colours chosen for the new concern were the old City of Cork white with black top, albeit with a red 'logo' on the side of the funnel. These colours survived until the introduction of the second generation of ro-ro ships in 1979/80.

Coast Lines ('Irish Coast')
    Hull black, upper-works white, funnel all black, with a large white V on each side.

THE ISLE OF MAN STEAM PACKET COMPANY

During the war years this concern, which had been founded in 1830, operated regular summer passenger services between Douglas and Liverpool, Fleetwood, Heysham, Ardrossan, Dublin and Belfast. Ramsey was served by certain of the Liverpool, Ardrossan and Belfast steamers. As well as the regular services there were many relief and excursion sailings which, on occasion, brought the company's ships to such additional ports as Barrow, Llandudno and Garlieston in Britain and (though rarely) Greenore in Ireland.

After the Second World War, during much of which regular passenger operations were restricted to one daily sailing each way between Douglas and Fleetwood, a reasonably extensive summer service was progressively introduced, though it never achieved the full extent of former days. The growth of air travel, the increasing availability of foreign holidays, together with improved, though costly, conditions of employment for the company's staff, and particularly for ships' officers and crews, were the main causes of the reduction in services.

Outside the holiday season, both before and after the Second World War, regular daily sailings operated for very many years between Liverpool and Douglas. Later Fleetwood became the main all the year round port. Cargo services were maintained between Douglas (and less frequently Peel) and Liverpool. For many years three small conventional vessels were employed, but

H S Corran

Rushen Castle, formerly the LNWR/LYR *Duke of Cornwall.* This ship was acquired by the IOMSP Co in 1928 and remained with them until sold for scrap in 1947. It is seen here at Douglas in 1936. She can be seen in her original guise on page 23.

The *Peel Castle* was originally built in 1894 as the *Duke of York* of the LNWR/LYR joint fleet. It was acquired by the IOMSP Co in 1912 and, apart from Admiralty service in the First World War, remained with the company until she was scrapped in 1938. The main dimensions of this little vessel were 1474 grt, length 310'2" and breadth 37'0".

IOMSP Co

for some time before the end of the company's independent existence two container vessels were used.

Many of the IOM passenger ships in use between 1919 and 1939 were elderly; some indeed had been acquired secondhand, mostly from railway companies. These older vessels included: *Mona's Queen*, a paddle steamer dating from 1885 and withdrawn in 1925, the last of her type to remain in the company's service; *Tynwald*, 1891-1930; *Manxman*, 1904-1949, an ex Midland Railway vessel purchased in 1919; *Viking*, 1905-54, a very fast ship which was often on the Belfast service in the early 1950s; *Victoria*, 1907-1957, a typical Denny-built railway steamer bought from the South Eastern and Chatham Railway in 1920, a ship which I frequently saw in Dublin in the early 1930s; *Rushen Castle*, 1898-1947, formerly the LYR/LNWR *Duke of Cornwall*, bought by the Isle of Man Company in 1928, also no stranger to Dublin in the 1930s; *Peel Castle*, 1894-1938, originally the *Duke of York*, which came to the Steam Packet Company in 1912; *Snaefell*, ex *Viper*, 1906-1945, bought from G and J Burns in 1920; *Douglas*, 1889-1923, originally the *Dora* of the London and South Western Railway Company, which changed hands as far back as 1901, and whose main claim to fame (or notoriety?), as an Isle of Man ship, stems from her having sunk after a collision in the Mersey, fortunately without loss of life; *Manx Maid*, 1910-1950, ex *Caesarea*, from the LSWR's Southampton-Channel Island fleet, which left the English Channel for the Irish Sea in 1923; *Mona's Isle*, built in 1905 as the *Onward* for the SECR, and *Ramsey Town*, which under her original name of *Antrim* has been referred to earlier.

Although I could claim to be on terms of nodding acquaintanceship with *Victoria* and *Rushen Castle*, dating from my pre-war peregrinations of the Dublin quays, and had at least observed *Viking* on Belfast Lough several times in the early 1950s, my knowledge of the other old stalwarts of the 1920s and 1930s was very slight, and I am greatly indebted to the compilers of *A Pictorial History of the Isle of Man Steam Packet Ships*, published in the company's 150th anniversary year of 1980, for much of the above information. I am equally indebted to my good friend Stan Corran, in his youth as much a devotee of the Isle of Man ships as I was of those of the B and I and the LMS, who gave me the booklet.

Despite the number of elderly vessels in the inter-war fleet, the Steam Packet did not entirely depend upon other firms cast offs during the 1930s. Three noteworthy ships were built, in 1927, 1930 and 1934, whilst 1936 saw the introduction of two more which, although each became a war casualty, had a considerable influence on the design of post-war replacements. The first three vessels may be considered together. *Ben my Chree* 1927, *Lady of Mann* 1930 and *Mona's Queen* 1934, were basically similar in appearance. Each had a counter stern (a somewhat old fashioned feature for the period), two tiers of promenade decks of which a considerable proportion was glassed in, and each carried five boats per side. Towards the end of the inter-war period all three ships were painted white. *Lady of Mann* and *Mona's Queen* appear to have been white from the start of their careers, whilst *Ben my Chree* received the treatment in 1932. The new ships all measured between 2500 and 3100 gross tons (the exact figures are listed below) and were powered by geared-turbines driving twin-screws. Each vessel was credited with having exceeded twenty-two knots on her trials. Here we may note that several of the firm's older ships had the earlier type of turbine installation, direct drive with triple-screws. The 'Three White Ladies of Douglas' (my own phrase), provided a standard of comfort considerably higher than that available in *Rushen Castle*, *Manx Maid* and their consorts. Judging from contemporary photographs the first class accommodation at any rate was fully up to the standards of the 1920s/30s railway steamers.

Lady of Mann and *Ben my Chree* survived the Second World War, during which they both saw hard and varied service, but the graceful *Mona's Queen* was lost at Dunkirk. Although this book does not deal specifically with the war service of the Irish Sea steamers, I think it may be mentioned that during the war *Ben my Chree* spent some time operating between Scotland and Iceland. We have already seen that *Lochgarry* (ex *Lairdsrock*) spent the last two years of her life on this route and that she met her end there. That, in all conscience, was an unlikely final employment and ultimate demise for the prosaic old 11 knot Belfast-Ardrossan plodder, but I have always felt that the use of the graceful white Isle

(Continued on page 137)

Barry Carse

Lady of Mann, built in 1930, at Sir John Rogerson's Quay, Dublin, about 1968. This ship was the last of the three 'White Ladies' and survived until 1971. At 3104 grt, she was the largest ship ever built for the Isle of Man Steam Packet Company.

Barry Carse

Mona's Isle, 2491 grt, built in 1951 by Cammell Laird, at the South Quays, Dublin, in 1979. This turbine steamer was one of the six post-war standard ships of the Isle of Man Steam Packet Company. Note the somewhat unusual black lifeboats.

Barry Carse

Manxman, 2495 grt, built at Cammell Laird's Birkenhead yard in 1955 — the last of the IOMSP Co's six post-war 'standard' ships. The photograph, taken in July 1969, shows the ship in the former traditional B and I passenger berth at North Wall, Dublin.

Barry Carse

Ben my Chree, 2762 grt, built in 1965, photographed at Douglas in September 1977. This, the last steam vessel to be acquired by the Isle of Man Steam Packet Company, was the firm's second ro-ro ship.

H S Corran

Ramsey Town of the Isle of Man Steam Packet Company. This photograph makes an interesting comparison with one of her on page 29, as the Midland Railway Company's *Antrim*.

of Man flier on such hard weather Atlantic duty was even more incongruous.

I never saw *Mona's Queen*. Occasionally I saw *Ben my Chree* in Belfast or making her way down the Lough, in the 1950s and early 1960s (she was not withdrawn until 1965). *Lady of Mann*, which survived until 1971, was also a sporadic visitor to Belfast, particularly during the days leading up to the July holiday period, and it is from this later time – in 1963 – that my abiding memory of this one time pride of the Isle of Man, and the largest ship ever built for her owners, dates.

I was travelling to Glasgow in Burns and Laird's *Royal Ulsterman* and at that time of year our departure at 2100 (9pm in those days) was in full daylight. *Lady of Mann* was lying alongside Donegall Quay, further down the river than the *Royal Ulsterman*'s berth. Presumably she was scheduled for an early sailing the next morning. The *Royal Ulsterman*, proceeding, according to regulation, dead slow, passed close alongside the Manx ship. From my stance on the boat deck I had an excellent view of the latter vessel. I was not impressed. However, *Lady of Mann* may have looked in her heyday, in all the glory of white paint and with the prestige of being her company's flagship, she now appeared old, not well cared for and in several places in need of paint. Eclipsed by the new standard post-war ships, this erstwhile pride of the fleet was now but a relic of a more gracious age, destined to serve out her remaining days on whatever route or schedule called for a maximum capacity ship, coping with the July holiday peak traffic from Belfast and Ardrossan, the August Bank Holiday excursion from

Dublin, or extra Friday night sailings from Liverpool at the height of summer.

So much for the three 'White Ladies'. In 1937, there appeared from the Vickers shipyard, Barrow-in-Furness, the sister ships *Tynwald* and *Fenella*, each of 2376 grt and measuring 314'6" and 46'1", which were designed specifically for the daily Douglas-Liverpool service outside the summer season. Although each of these was lost during the war (*Fenella* at Dunkirk and *Tynwald* off the coast of Algeria), the pair may be regarded as the precursors of the series of very successful post-war additions to the Steam Packet's fleet. These six: *King Orry*, the first to be built, *Snaefell*, *Mona's Queen*, *Tynwald*, *Mona's Isle* and *Manxman*, the last in the series, appeared between 1946 and 1955 and, although there were some individual differences, they were all generally similar with the important exception that *Manxman* broke new ground as regards main engines. Whilst each of the other five ships had a conventional twin-screw geared-turbine installation, *Manxman* was fitted with Pamtrada turbines of an advanced design. These turbines took steam from the boilers at a pressure of 385lb per square inch, compared to the 250lb of the other standard ships.

The six standard ships were the mainstay of the Steam Packet's services for many years but like other vessels of their generation (the 1956 Heysham-Belfast 'Dukes' are a prime example), they were overtaken by the ro-ro revolution and were outdated long before they had become worn out. Indeed, bearing in mind that the average IOMSP Co passenger ship spent more time each year laid up than it did in service (due to the highly seasonal nature of the company's business) the post-war standard vessels might, but for the ro-ros, have lasted well into the 1990s. As things were, however, they had all gone by 1982. *Manxman*, the last of them, was sold and subsequently scrapped in 1982.

The relatively light use of the company's ships was of course a factor in prolonging the lives of many of the veteran steamers of the 1920s and 1930s. Even if one makes a generous allowance for the intensity of use during the summer, the average annual period of activity of an Isle of Man passenger ship would not have exceeded the equivalent of six months work by a comparable railway or Coast Lines vessel.

I have just referred to ro-ros. As will be seen, the company introduced this class of ship, though only one at a time, in the 1960s and early 1970s. Until all four drive-on/drive-off vessels were in service, and so long as any of the standard ships were still operating, the well established practice of carrying a limited number of motor vehicles on deck persisted. The number of cars which could be accommodated on a sailing was of course severely limited and the time taken in the embarkation and disembarkation process did not endear itself to passengers. In view of the renowned series of motor cycle races in the island in late spring and early autumn, the carriage of motor cycles, a relatively easy process, had long been a feature of the Steam Packet's activities.

The first of the ro-ro ships, *Manx Maid* and *Ben my Chree* (a time honoured name) appeared in 1962 and 1965 respectively. As was the case with British Rail/Sealink's *Caledonian Princess*, *Holyhead Ferry One* and other contemporary vessels, the Isle of Man Company was not yet prepared to forsake the steam turbine and so both of the new ships were given Pamtrada turbine machinery — trial speeds in each case were around the 22 knot mark. These somewhat chunky looking vessels used the ingenious but, in some respects restrictive, type of embarkation equipment for vehicles which has already been described. Car deck capacity was ninety cars or small commercial vehicles.

The next, and last two ro-ro vessels to be built for the Steam Packet in its days as an independent company, did not appear until the 1970s and hence, strictly speaking, do not fall to be considered here. However, if for no other reason than that the pair were the only IOMSP Co ships in which I ever travelled, perhaps they deserve a mention.

The first of the new ships — *Mona's Queen*, 2998 grt, 104.45m x 16.74m, which appeared in 1971, was noteworthy in two respects. She was the first post-war vessel for the company not to have been built by Cammel Laird's Birkenhead yard. She came from the Ailsa Shipbuilding Company of Troon. She was also the IOMSP Co's pioneer diesel-engined ship. Power was provided by Crossley Pielstick engines driving twin variable-pitch propellers, with direct control from the bridge. Other mechanical features included a bow thruster and stabilisers.

The last of the vehicle carriers to appear during the IOMSP Co's independent existence was *Lady of Mann*, 2290 grt, 104.43m x 16.74m. This vessel, also built at Troon by the Ailsa Shipbuilding Co, was similar to *Mona's Queen* in most respects, including the combination of main mast and exhaust pipe (one could scarcely call it a funnel). This feature, with what appeared to be a normal funnel, being a dummy, had become fairly common in Scandinavian vessels but had not, as far as I remember, appeared before on the Irish Sea, except in the case of the Viking vessels and the *Stena Nordica*. The B and I ro-ros of 1968/69, *Munster*, *Leinster* and *Innisfallen*, did incorporate main mast and exhaust facility in one structure but in the form of a conventional streamlined funnel with a mast mounted in its leading rim.

Since my experiences of travelling in Isle of Man ships comprises just three passages, all in ro-ros (a return trip between Dublin and Douglas in *Lady of Mann* and the already described Holyhead-Dublin journey in *Mona's Queen*) I can say very little about either of these ships. I can state, however, that in both of them the one class passenger accommodation struck me as being no more attractive than the somewhat spartan facilities of the first B and I ro-ros for the transport of private cars and small commercial vehicles. Only the Steam Packet was turning its back on the growing traffic in road freight. This fact became all too apparent at the end of the 1970s, when the multi purpose ro-ro ship *Manx Viking*, operated by an independent company, Manx Line, commenced operations between Heysham and Douglas. This development was soon followed by the new company being effectively taken over by Sealink and, eventually, by the time honoured Isle of Man Steam Packet Company itself passing to Sealink's control.

Once Sealink became established as the major force driving the island company, it was only a matter of time, and a short time at that, before *Ben my Chree* and *Manx Maid* were declared redundant. Sealink had no lack of suitable vessels with which to maintain a fully comprehensive, permanent freight and passenger connection with the island and so, after languishing in Birkenhead docks for some time, open to offers to purchase which no one seemed to wish to make, the Steam Packet's two pioneer car ferries went to the breakers yard in the mid 1980s. For some time Sealink maintained its all year round island service with *Manx Viking* and various other ships but, in 1990, the erstwhile *Saint Eloi* (subsequently named *Channel Entente*), which had been built for the Dover-Dunkirk train ferry route, was given a major refit and transferred to the Isle of Man service under the name of *King Orry*. Previously, in 1989, *Lady of Mann* had also been refitted and she was retained for the summer services to ports without linkspans.

It is good that the name of the old company has been retained, even though the concern is now part of the Stena multi-national empire. There have been many changes since the loss of independence and there will be more. Just as the conventional ships were superseded by the first ro-ros, and these in turn have given way to larger and more versatile craft, so we are now seeing further development on the Irish Sea and elsewhere with the advent of fast catamaran services.

No doubt there will continue to be plenty to interest future chroniclers of the ships and operations of the IOMSP Co and other companies. Your octogenarian author – a steam man (albeit a lay one) and a devotee of the reciprocating and the turbine engine – though he remains keenly interested in passenger services on the Irish Sea, realises his limitations and gladly leaves the recording of current and future events to younger writers.

ISLE OF MAN STEAM PACKET COMPANY - *Passenger ships, July 1939*

Ben my Chree	1927	2586 grt	The first of the three 'White Ladies'.
Fenella	1937	2376 grt	Prototype for the post-war standard ships. Lost at Dunkirk.
King Orry	1913	1877 grt	Served in two World Wars. Lost at Dunkirk.
Lady of Mann	1930	3104 grt	One of the 'White Ladies'; the largest ship ever built for the company. Lasted until 1971.
Manxman	1904	2030 grt	A former Midland Railway ship acquired after the First World War.
Manx Maid	1910	1504 grt	Formerly the LSWR *Caesarea*
Mona's Isle	1905	1688 grt	Formerly the SECR *Onward*
Mona's Queen	1934	2755 grt	The third 'White Lady'. Lost at Dunkirk.
Rushen Castle	1898	1724 grt	Ex LNWR/LYR *Duke of Cornwall*. Together with *Snaefell* she maintained the service to the IOM during the Second World War.

Snaefell	1906	1713 grt		Formerly the *Viper* of G and J Burns.
Tynwald	1937	2375 grt		Sister ship to *Fenella*. Lost off the coast of Algeria during the Second World War.
Victoria	1907	1641 grt		A former SECR vessel. Acquired in 1920.
Viking	1905	1957 grt		The company's forst turbine steamer. Evacuated children from Guernsey in 1940.

Withdrawal dates of vessels which survived the Second World War

Ben my Chree	1965	*Lady of Mann*	1971	*Manxman*	1949
Manx Maid	1950	*Mona's Isle*	1947	*Rushen Castle*	1947
Snaefell	1945	*Victoria*	1957	*Viking*	1957

The six standard ships of the Isle of Man Steam Packet Company

King Orry	1946	2485 grt	345'1" x 47'2"	Fourth ship of the name.
Tynwald	1947	2493 grt	344'10" x 47'5"	Fifth ship to bear this name.
Mona's Queen	1947	2485 grt	345'0" x 47'2"	Fourth of the name. Sold in 1962 and became Epirotiki lines *Fiesta*.
Snaefell	1948	2489 grt	344'10" x 47'2"	Fifth ship of the name.
Mona's Isle	1951	2491 grt	345'0" x 47'2"	Fourth ship of the name.
Manxman	1955	2495 grt	344'10" x 50'0"	Second of the name and last survivor of the sextet. Fitted with 'Pamtrada'* turbines and high pressure boilers.

*Pamtrada

This word, denoting the type of machinery fitted to the second *Manxman*, and also to the ro-ro vessels *Ben my Chree* and *Manx Maid*, is an acronym from the words 'Parsons and Marine Turbine Research and Development Association'.

Hull and funnel colours

With the exception of the three 'White Ladies', hull colours for all vessels, both before and after the Second World War, were black with white upperworks. Some vessels had black lifeboats, others had brown boats with, so far as could be ascertained from the quayside, a high gloss varnish finish. To my knowledge it was only the six standard vessels which had other than white boats. Funnels were red with black tops and two narrow black lines evenly dividing the space below the black top. This pattern of funnel colour was an exact copy of the Cunard company's style. It may well have predated the latter since the Isle of Man concern was already ten years old by the time *Britannia*, the first Cunarder, appeared in 1840. During the Second World War, ships were painted in all over grey.

RO-RO VESSELS, 1969

By the year 1969 ro-ro ships were operating on all remaining routes of BR/Sealink and of the erstwhile Coast Lines, whilst the Isle of Man Steamship Company had acquired its first two vessels of the type. Even on the Dun Laoghaire-Holyhead service, where the *Hibernia* and *Cambria* of 1949 still operated the main services, *Holyhead Ferry One* not only maintained a ro-ro service during the summer season but had taken over *Princess Maud's* role as a standby and relief ship for the traditional vessels during the rest of the year.

The list below names the regular ro-ro passenger ships which operated on BR and ex Coast Line routes in the summer of 1969, together with the pioneer Isle of Man vessels which, on account of their unique loading and unloading arrangements, could operate in any of their owners' services. I have used the phrase 'regular ro-ro passenger ships' since, in the case of the BR routes, vessels could be and were interchanged, not only between the Irish Sea services, but also between these and those across the English Channel. A notable example of this practice was the frequency with which *Holyhead Ferry One* and her sister vessel *Dover*, exchanged roles and home ports. However, in 1969 *Holyhead Ferry One* operated the service for which she had been designed. Full details of all ships listed have already been given, so, to avoid repetition, only names and building dates are noted here.

SEALINK SERVICES

Larne-Stranraer
TSS *Caledonian Princess*   1962
TSMV *Antrim Princess*   1967

Belfast-Heysham
TSS *Duke of Lancaster*   1956
TSS *Duke of Argyll*   1956

Dun Laoghaire-Holyhead
TSS *Holyhead Ferry One*   1966

Rosslare-Fishguard
TSS *Saint David*   1947
TSS *Duke of Rothesay*   1956

Notes:

1 *Duke of Lancaster*, *Duke of Argyll*, *Duke of Rothesay* and *Saint David* were all conversions of traditional ships

2 The stern loading ro-ro ship *Holyhead Ferry One*, 3879grt, was in 1976 fitted with bow loading facilities, renamed *Earl Leofric*, and transferred permanently to Dover. The vessel was sold for scrap in 1981, when only sixteen years old.

FORMER COAST LINES SERVICES

Belfast-Liverpool
TSMV *Ulster Prince*   1967
TSMV *Ulster Queen*   1967

Belfast- Ardrossan
TSMV *Lion*   1968

Dublin- Liverpool
TSMV *Leinster*   1969
TSMV *Munster*   1968

Cork-Swansea
TSMV *Innisfallen*   1969

Notes:

1 The British and Irish Steam Packet Company was acquired from Coast Lines in 1966 by the Irish Government.

2 The Belfast Steamship Company, Burns and Laird Lines and other Coast Lines subsidiaries were acquired by P and O (the Peninsular and Oriental Steamship Company) in 1968.

3 Strictly speaking, Cork-Swansea was never a Coast Lines route. It was not opened until 1969. However, since it was a replacement of the former Cork-Fishguard operation, it is reasonable for it to be listed here.

ISLE OF MAN STEAM PACKET COMPANY SERVICES

Available for all routes.
TSMV *Manx Maid*   1962
TSMV *Ben my Chree*   1965

Note:

Although the above two vessels were, in theory, available to operate on any of the Company's routes, in practice they were largely confined to the Liverpool-Douglas service until the advent of two more ro-ros, *Mona's Queen* and *Lady of Mann*, in 1971 and 1975 respectively. Neither Fleetwood nor Dublin, for example, had a ro-ro service to Douglas until after the advent of *Mona's Queen*.

EPILOGUE

So much for 'conventional' passenger services across the Irish Sea. Beginning in the late 1960s, there came larger, but fewer, ships and the long losing fight against the aircraft began. In the 1970s, the ro-ro vessels stabilised the situation but at the cost of the closure of several routes and the further reduction in the number of ships. Now the railways have no vessels on the Irish Sea and Coast Lines is just a memory. Such of the erstwhile railway routes as remain are operated by Stena. Just recently, the last of the old company titles, the British and Irish Steam Packet Company, though disassociated from Coast Lines since 1967, has disappeared. What was the B and I, is now a section of Irish Ferries, itself a part of the Irish Continental Group.

I began this account of services and travel across the Irish Sea with a less than flattering reference to the *Lairdsmoor*. I would like, however, to recall another memory of the same ship — a memory of rising early on a summer morning, after a night passage from Dublin to Glasgow, and making my way to the open deck on a level with, and immediately aft of, the bridge. Ahead, and to port, were the green mountains of Kintail, to starboard lay Gourock with its fleet of Caledonian Steam Packet Company (LMS) paddlers. Just before the *Lairdsmoor* turned to starboard to enter the mouth of the Clyde, preparatory to the call at Greenock, the big two funnelled LNER paddler *Jeanie Deans* passed on our port side, the foam churned up by her wheels sparkling in the sunshine. On her after deck a solitary piper saluted the morning of a perfect summer day.

Led by the aroma of frying bacon which, at this busy time for the galley staff, was easily discernible above the competing odours from the cattle pens, I descended to the saloon to snatch a hasty breakfast whilst the ship was alongside the Greenock quay. Still to come was the two hour passage up the Clyde, an experience never to be missed, with the highlights of the first hour being Dumbarton Rock and its memories of the *Comet* (the world's first steamship), and the venerable MacBrayne paddler *Columba* and the smaller Williamson Buchanan *Kylemore* or *Queen Empress*, each crowded with day trippers going 'doon the watter'. Later there would be one, or perhaps two, Anchor liners at their regular berth on the north side of the river, and the call at Merklands wharf nearby. What would be seen in the way of Blue Funnel, Clan, Ellerman, Henderson or Harrison liners was hard to predict, but it would have been a disappointing day if representatives of at least four of these companies were not in port or proceeding down the river. Finally the Broomielaw, terminus of the crossing, with its collection of Burns Laird and MacBrayne vessels, and, immediately across the river, ships of the Clyde and Sloan companies.

The largely idle shipyards along the river banks struck a sad note, but the full social and economic consequences of their desolation was scarcely realised by an eighteen year old from a comfortable middle class background. With maturer years would come greater understanding of the tragedy of the Great Depression and also of the part played by long hours, low wages and cheap coal in the development of cross channel services.

Finally, and to balance my recollection of a pre-war journey, here is a brief account of a more recent one, admittedly in a ro-ro vessel but nevertheless one that I am unlikely to forget.

I must have made at least one hundred and fifty return journeys by sea between Ireland and Britain, in at least fifty different ships. The majority of these crossings took place between 1949 and 1988, but around thirty-five between 1915 and 1945. Since September 1989 I have lived in Australia, once a leading nation as regards coastal passenger shipping, but which now has only one major passenger service, that between mainland Australia and Tasmania. On our return trips to Ireland my wife and I, as befits elderly grandparents with luggage and without a car, cross the Irish Sea by air, a pleasurable enough experience for anyone who, like myself, is interested in almost any form of transport (I draw the line at ski lifts and roller blades), but a far cry from the *Lairdsmoor*, the *Saint Andrew*, or even the vomit inducing *Lairdsford*. The reader may therefore imagine what pleasure I experienced when we boarded the *Duchesse Anne* of Brittany Ferries at Portsmouth in May 1993, having just established that the vessel was indeed, as I had hardly dared to hope, our old friend the *Connacht* of 1979 which had carried us and our car many times between Dublin and Liverpool in the 1980s, and in which my wife had accompanied several school parties. The B and I had sold the *Connacht* to Brittany Ferries in 1988, after Holyhead became the terminal in Britain for their night as well as day passenger service ex-Dublin, thus enabling both operations to be carried out with one ship. There had also been compelling financial factors behind this sale.

However, it is not either of our passages to and from Saint Malo which I wish to record as my final memory of travelling in an Irish Sea passenger vessel, but one of rather greater relevance to the theme of this book.

On a wild midwinter day in the early 1980s, my wife and I, returning from a Christmas visit to our second son and his family in the English Midlands, arrived at the Liverpool dockside preparatory to embarking for the 1200 B and I sailing to Dublin. I do not know just what the wind force was, but it was raising sheets of spray from the normally placid surface of the water of the enclosed dock. This was discouraging, but far worse was the fact that there was no ship for us to board. Since she normally berthed at around 0700, the omens for our getting home that night were scarcely auspicious.

However the *Connacht* eventually appeared, some five hours late, and, in due course, we drove on board. During our long wait, we had for a while left the car and repaired to the 'foot passengers'' waiting area. (I have yet to see a footless passenger in a B and I or any other ship.) Here we got into conversation with a lady who was travelling to Ireland at short notice because of some family emergency. This good soul was more than a little nervous at the prospect of crossing in such bad weather, so we spent some time reassuring her that, in due course, the ship would appear and that we would arrive in Dublin unscathed, even if somewhat late. I must admit that, even whilst I was painting such a rosy picture for the lone traveller, I was forming a mental image of the vessel still sheltering under the lee of the Isle of Man, or at best riding out the blow in the outer reaches of Liverpool Bay.

In the event, by the time we had cleared the Mersey entrance, the wind had moderated considerably and we had a pleasant enough crossing, during which we paid a long overdue visit to the cafeteria. On our way out of this apartment we encountered our apprehensive fellow traveller, cheerfully chatting with a third party. On enquiring of the good lady how she felt, and inwardly congratulating ourselves that our optimistic forecast of conditions on the journey had been borne out, she replied: "This is great, it's just like being in a supermarket!" (No doubt she was referring to the duty free facilities.) A supermarket! — shades of the bullocks in the 'tween decks of the *Lairdsford* with their heads almost over the counter of the third class bar! That woman never knew what real cross channel travel was about.

World Ship Society

The British and Irish Steam Packet Company's motor ship *Connacht* , 6812 grt, 122.03m x 18.60m, delivered to the company by Verolme Dockyard, Cork, in the autumn of 1979. This ship was sold to Brittany Ferries in 1988. After making some alterations to her accomodation, her new owners renamed the ship *Duchesse Anne* and employed her on the Portsmouth-St Malo route. In her B and I days a passenger paid the *Connacht* the doubtful compliment of likening her to a supermarket. The *Leinster*, built by Verlome in 1980, was a virtual sister ship to the *Connacht*. However her grt was 6807 and there were certain differences between the Atlas diesel engines of the two ships, resulting in the *Leinster* being credited with a service speed of 21 knots, whilst that of the *Connacht* was twenty.

GLOSSARY OF NAUTICAL TERMS

**Amidships,
or 'midships**   The central part of a ship.

Aft, or After   Towards the rear of a vessel.

Catamaran   A vessel with two hulls placed parallel to one another, and upon which the superstructure is built.

Coaming   A raised edge to a hatch (see below) or other opening in a ship, to prevent the ingress of water.

Counter stern   A traditionally shaped stern of a ship, overhanging the water.

Cruiser stern   A design of stern without any overhang. This pattern originated in warships in order to avoid exposing the rudder to hostile gunfire.

Davits   Small cranes used for lowering and hoisting a ship's lifeboats.

**Foreward,
or forward**   Designates the fore or front part of a ship. Sometimes spelt **for'ard**.

Forecastle   Sometimes written **fo'csle**. A raised structure at the extreme fore end of a ship. The term was also sometimes used to denote crews' or passengers' accommodation right up in the bows of a vessel, even in cases where there was no raised structure.

Hatch   An opening in a ship's deck giving access to a hold.

GRT   An abbreviation for **Gross Registered Tonnage**. This has nothing to do with weight, but is a measure of a ship's capacity. In the case of most of the vessels mentioned in this book a gross ton was one hundred cubic feet of permanently enclosed space, less the space necessary for the operation of the vessel, ie: officers' and crews' accommodation, engine room, store rooms etc. In practice various rules applied for the calculation of gross tonnage which might exempt certain spaces, even though these could well be categorised as revenue earning.

Link Span   An adjustable gangway which enables vehicles to be driven onto or off a ro-ro (see below) ship, irrespective of the height of the tide.

MS   Short for **Motor Ship**.

MV   Short for **Motor Vessel**.

Poop   A raised structure at the after end of a vessel.

Port, or portside   The left hand side of a ship, looking foreward.

Purser   The officer in charge of a passenger vessel's accounts and also (usually in co-operation with the Chief Steward) of the catering and other domestic arrangements.

Ro-ro   Short for **roll on-roll off**, indicating a ship onto or off which vehicles may be driven, without the need to use cranes or other gear.

Starboard   The right had side of a ship, looking foreward.

SS   Frequently thought to be an abbreviation for the words 'steam ship', but originally the letters were short for the words **Screw Steamer**.

TSS   **Twin Screw Steamer**, or ship. Hence also **TSMV** and **TSMS**.

TrSS   **Triple Screw Steamer** or ship.

Washports   Openings in a ship's side to enable water on a deck to be discharged into the sea, but which also impede the entrance of more water.

INDEX OF SHIPS

*(Figures in **bold type** indicate illustrations.)*

Notes:
Dates in brackets in the index are the dates of entering service. Where more than one name is given, the additional names are for the name **immediately previous** or the one **immediately after** the first name: eg *Ulster Prince, ex Leinster (1937)/Adria* means that **Ulster Prince** previously **was** the *Leinster* and **became** the *Adria*.

Rear cover
Scottish Coast, 3817 grt, built by Harland and Wolff in 1957, leaving Donegall Quay, Belfast in the late 1960s. It is probably on a Burns and Lairds summer 'daylight' service to Ardrossan.

Brian Boyle